Good Housekeep

ESSENTIAL
FOOD PROCESSOR
HANDBOOK

Good Housekeeping

ESSENTIAL
FOOD PROCESSOR
HANDBOOK

All you need to know to make the most of your machine,
with over 100 recipes

EBURY PRESS
LONDON

First published in 1996

1 3 5 7 9 10 8 6 4 2

First published in the United Kingdom in 1996 by
Ebury Press Random House, 20 Vauxhall Bridge Road,
London SW1V 2SA

Random House Australia (Pty) Limited
20 Alfred Street, Milsons Point, Sydney,
New South Wales 2061, Australia

Random House New Zealand Limited
18 Poland Road, Glenfield, Auckland 10, New Zealand

Random House·South Africa (Pty) Limited
PO Box 337, Bergvlei, South Africa

Random House UK Limited Reg. No. 954009

A catalogue record for this book is available from the
British Library.

ISBN 0 09 181342 5

Editor: Jennie Shapter
Design: Paul Wood
Introductory text: Jennie Shapter
New recipes: Joanna Farrow, Jennnie Shapter, Patricia Stone

Printed and bound in Great Britain by
BPC Books Limited.

Contents

Introduction

One of the most useful electrical appliances developed to make food preparation quick and easy is the food processor. If you have owned one for some time you will probably have found out how many of the previously laborious food preparation chores can now be carried out within seconds and without any physical effort. A food processor can take the place of many other gadgets in the kitchen. It will perform most of the basic tasks required when preparing food, from mixing, blending, whisking and kneading to puréeing, grating, slicing and chopping.

When you first buy a food processor, or update your existing model, make sure you familiarize yourself with the machine and how the accessories work, before you start to cook, as each food processor has its own particular features. Also make sure you check the maximum volume the machine can handle. Some machines will only handle 500 g (1 lb) of bread dough whilst others will cope with up to 1.4 kg (3 lb). By adding more than the machine is designed for will overload the motor and could damage it. Likewise some machines have a maximum liquid capacity of 600 ml (1 pint) whilst others have in excess of 2 litres (3½ pints). If you are purchasing a new machine make sure the processor you select will handle the volumes you are likely to make.

It is a good idea to place your food processor in a central position in the kitchen so that it is always ready for use. If you put it in a cupboard it will tend to stop you making the best use of it. Some models come with a plastic cover to stop them collecting dust. Keep all the attachments near the machine either in the rack supplied by the manufacturer, or in a drawer or cupboard, so they are close to hand, ready for use.

This handbook includes a good selection of recipes which show how the food processor can help you save both time and effort. Don't limit yourself to these recipes, but use the methods as a guideline and adapt your favourite recipes.

FEATURES AND ATTACHMENTS

Food processors vary from one manufacturer to another and from model to model, but usually include most, if not all of the following:

Processor Bowl and Lid with Feed Tube: The bowl will vary in size from model to model. If you have a large family, or prepare large quantities of food, then opt for a larger capacity bowl. It is also worth considering purchasing a spare bowl to save washing up the same bowl when making several dishes, or switching from savoury to sweet dishes.

A plastic spatula, which will not scratch, is provided to scrape down the mixture from the sides of the bowl.

Some bowls have a liquid level mark to check the quantity and ensure you do not exceed the maximum. If the bowl does not have a mark keep the liquid level below the top of the central spindle.

Some processors are fitted with a mini-bowl and blade which fits inside the main bowl. This is ideal for chopping or blending small quantities.

Pusher for Feed Tube: The pusher is shaped to fit the feed tube. It must always be used to help feed food into the food processor when slicing or grating. Never use your fingers or a piece of equipment apart from the pusher; the blades are extremely sharp.

Some machines have two feed tubes and pushers, one larger than the other, or one feed tube with a two piece pusher, where the centre section is removable. These two sizes allow different shapes of food and small quantities to be accommodated. Thin items such as courgettes, carrots and bananas are best fed through the narrower feed tube for slicing.

Most manufacturers also include a liquid measure indicator in millilitres and fluid ounces on the pusher.

Metal Blade: This double bladed knife is the basic attachment which comes with every food processor. It is extremely sharp and will happily tackle all the chopping, puréeing, blending and mixing tasks. Use it to chop vegetables, nuts, herbs, meat and fish, to make breadcrumbs, cakes and pastry and to purée soups, sauces and fruits.

Dough Blade or Hook: This attachment is for kneading bread doughs. It varies in design, some manufacturers include a plastic blade, similar to the metal blade, but made in plastic, without any sharp edges, whilst others provide a metal hook. A continental style metal dough tool, which is more suited to making continental style yeast doughs such as rye bread and stollen, is an optional extra with some machines.

Slicing Disc: Some machines have a selection of slicing discs as standard, whilst with others there is only one and other sizes are optional extras. Where you have only one disc, you must use different amounts of pressure on the pusher to achieve thinner or thicker slices, this of course, does have its limitations.

Most machines have a standard 3-4 mm slicing blade fitted to the disc. Other sizes which are either standard or optional are 2 mm and 6 mm.

Grating Disc: Grating discs, like slicing discs vary with each machine. Most food processors come with a choice of at least two sizes. The most common are a fine 3 mm grating hole and a medium 5 mm grating hole. Some manufacturers include a very coarse 8 mm grater which can be used to prepare thin sticks of vegetables for stir-frying or salads, instead of using a stir-fry or fine chipper disc.

A very fine grater for extra hard cheese, such as Parmesan cheese is also available as an optional extra with some food processors.

Chipper/Stir-fry Disc: This disc is designed to take the chore out of making potato chips. Sizes vary between 7-12 mm. The smaller sizes obviously make thinner chips, which also makes these discs suitable for preparing vegetables such as carrot, turnip, courgette, beetroot and cucumber for stir-frying and salads. The 12 mm slicer gives traditional British sized chips.

Whisk: One of the criticisms of food processors in the past has been their inability to successfully whisk foods, such as egg whites and cream. Now special whisking tools are available as standard with most machines. Some include a balloon shaped whisk which may be plastic or fine metal, others include a paddle blade.

Slightly less volume may be achieved whisking egg whites and cream in the food processor, but it still gives a good result and can be used for soufflés, meringues and desserts or cakes with whipped cream. To obtain the best results when whipping egg whites, leave the food pusher out of the feed tube to allow a flow of air into the food processor bowl.

Do not use the whisk for heavier mixes, the metal blade should be used. If in doubt, consult your manufacturer's handbook.

Citrus Press: This piece of equipment will quickly squeeze the juice from oranges, limes, lemons and grapefruits. It will extract the maximum amount of juice possible with little effort. Ideal for large quantities of fruit juice, such as freshly squeezed orange for breakfast.

Optional Extras: There is a wide choice of optional extras available, the exact items will vary with different food processors. Juice extractors, suitable for hard fruits and vegetables, a potato peeler, a flour sieve, different sizes of grating and slicing discs and a julienne disc are just some of the extras available. Some manufacturers now provide a food processor, liquidiser and mixer in one machine, to give the best possible piece of equipment for the job. This may be worth considering if you need to update other pieces of equipment. Other options include a liquidiser and food processor in one, to ensure extra fine puréeing, and a multi-mill attachment for very small quantities.

Controls: Some machines are fitted with a variable speed control, to help guard against over-processing. Use the lower speeds for slicing, grating, whisking and cake making and the higher speeds for chopping, yeast mixtures and puréeing. It is a good idea to start on a low speed when chopping foods so you can check what stage the food has reached and so avoid over-chopping. Many machines have a pulse control. This will only activate the machine whilst the switch is pressed and held in position. This feature allows greater control over the final texture of the food being processed. Use for rough chopping and mixing to avoid over-blending.

SAFETY

Food processors have a built-in safety lock to ensure that the sharp blades and discs cannot accidently be operated. The bowl and lid must be correctly engaged before the machine will operate. Most machines which have on and off buttons will only allow the lid to be removed when the control is in the off position. However even those machines where the lid can be turned whilst the control button is still in the on position immediately disengage the motor and blade or disc. There are several general points of safety which should be noted:

● Do not remove the lid until the rotating parts come to a full stop.

● Keep the pushers in the feed tubes unless they are being used, or egg whites are being whisked.

● Always use the pusher to guide food down the feed tube.

● Never put your fingers or an implement, such as the spatula in the feed tubes whilst the food processor is operating.

● Do not leave the food processor unattended whilst it is switched on.

● Do not allow children to operate the appliance unless supervised.

● Take care when handling the metal blades and slicing discs as they are very sharp.

● Every food processor has a maximum quantity which is safe to process. If you exceed the bowl capacity with liquids they may leak from the processor bowl. Apart from being messy, it could damage the motor. Exceeding the recommended quantities is likely to give poor results and could strain the motor.

TECHNIQUES

The food processor is extremely simple to use, but can take you by surprise to begin with by the speed at which it works. As with most pieces of equipment, to get the best results it is important to use it correctly. Follow the guidelines below to obtain the best results.

METAL BLADE
CHOPPING

The metal blade will chop hard and soft foods. To obtain an even result when chopping, pre-chop the food into equal sized pieces. Place the food in the processor bowl and switch on. For the best results when chopping, turn the food processor on twice, rather than once. Use the pulse button to roughly chop meat, fish, fruit, nuts and vegetables.

CHEESE: To chop hard cheese, such as Parmesan, cut into 2.5 cm (1 inch) cubes and drop down the feed tube with the motor running. Check every 5 seconds, until the desired size is achieved. Process softer, hard cheeses using the grating disc. Do not keep the motor running too long or the cheese could become warm and turn lumpy.

CRUMBS: Bread can easily be crumbed. Avoid very fresh bread as it tends to cling together in a doughy mass. Cut or tear into 2.5-5 cm (1-2 inch) pieces and process for 10-15 seconds or until crumbed. Biscuits can also be briefly processed to produce a crumb, for cheesecake and dessert bases.

FISH: Remove the skin and bones from raw fish and cut into 2.5 cm (1 inch) cubes. Check every 5-10 seconds until the desired texture is achieved.

HERBS: Make sure the bowl, blade and herbs are dry. Remove any coarse stalks. A larger quantity gives the best results. For small quantities use the mini-bowl or multi-mill attachment. Left-over chopped herbs can be stored, covered, in the refrigerator for a couple of days.

MEAT: Remove any gristle, bone and excess fat from raw meat. Cut into 2.5 cm (1 inch) cubes and then process as for fish.

MUSHROOMS: Make sure they are all of a similar size. large, cut into smaller pieces. Take care not to over-process, it will only take 4-5 seconds to chop mushrooms.

NUTS: Use only shelled nuts, process preferably on pulse setting for a few seconds only to coarsely chop. Process for 20-30 seconds to finely grind.

ONIONS: Peel and quarter, then place in the processor bowl and process for 5-10 seconds, depending on the quantity. Take care not to over-chop.

PURÉEING

FRUIT: Soft fruits can be processed raw. Hull or remove any stalks. Large fruits such as peaches and mangoes must be stoned, peeled if necessary and cut into smaller pieces first. Process for 5-10 seconds, or until a purée forms. Hard fruits such as apples, pears, apricots and plums need to be stoned or cored and cooked in a little sugar syrup until tender. Drain off any excess liquid and then process as for soft fruits.

VEGETABLES: Cooked vegetables such as carrots, swede, cauliflower and Brussels sprouts will all form a purée which can be mixed with a little butter and milk or yogurt and seasoning. Tomatoes can be quartered and then processed to a purée or skinned and de-seeded, then briefly processed to give chopped tomatoes.

SOUPS: When puréeing soup, add the vegetables first and process to a purée, then with the machine switched on, gradually add the liquid through the feed tube.

MIXING

BATTER: Batter mixes for pancakes, Yorkshire puddings and fritters are easy to make. Add half the liquid and the dry ingredients to the food processor bowl and process for a few seconds until smooth. Gradually add the remaining liquid through the feed tube.

CAKES: For best results use the all-in-one method and place all the ingredients in the food processor bowl. Only process for a few seconds until the ingredients are combined. If using butter or hard margarine, make sure it is softened first.

MAYONNAISE AND ROUILLE: Place the egg yolks, seasoning and half the vinegar in the food processor then with the machine running gradually add the oil and remaining vinegar through the feed tube. Continue processing until emulsified.

MILK SHAKES: Place the milk, fruit and a little sugar to taste in the food processor bowl and process for 5-10 seconds to blend. Add a scoop of ice-cream with the milk and fruit for an extra frothy milk shake.

PASTRY: Cut the fat into small pieces. Process the flour and fat until the mixture resembles fine breadcrumbs. Add the liquid through the feed tube and process until a pastry ball is formed.

VINAIGRETTE DRESSINGS AND MARINADES: Place all the ingredients in the food processor bowl and process for

20-30 seconds until combined and any herbs are chopped.

SLICING DISC

Ideally two different slicing thicknesses will give the best results, so if your food processor only has one it may be worth investing in another. If a recipe specifies a thinner or thicker slicing disc to the one you have, don't worry, it should not affect the end result greatly. If vegetables are cooked after slicing, the timing may alter slightly if they are thinner or thicker than stated.

It is important to fill the feed tube evenly and to cut any large foods to fit, for the best results. Think about the way cut foods are positioned to obtain the correct shapes. If processing large amounts, empty the bowl from time to time.

BANANAS: Peel and place upright in the feed tube. Use the smaller feed tube, if available, for one banana.

CABBAGE: Trim and remove the core. Cut into quarters or eighths to fit the feed tube and place upright.

CARROTS: Fill the entire feed tube with carrots to prevent them from slipping. Use the smaller feed tube, where available, for smaller quantities and small carrots. Process uncooked carrots and place them vertically in the feed tube. Cut in half, if longer than the feed tube.

COURGETTES: Process as for carrots.

CUCUMBER: Use a thin slicing disc, if available. Choose a small cucumber which will fit whole into the feed tube. Cut it flat across the bottom before placing in the feed tube.

LEEKS: Process as for carrots.

MUSHROOMS: Place the mushrooms, horizontally, one on top of another to fill the feed tube. Press lightly with the pusher.

ONIONS: Peel and quarter, or halve if small. The medium slicing disc is ideal. To slice spring onions, cut in half and fill the entire feed tube with onions, to prevent them from slipping. Use the smaller feed tube, where available.

PEARS: Select short, firm but ripe pears. Cut in half or quarters, depending on size and remove the pips and core. If possible place horizontally in the feed tube to give a pear shaped slice.

PEPPERS: Cut peppers into two halves and remove the core and seeds. Fold each half into itself and place vertically in the feeder tube. Place one pepper on top of another. Use the medium or thick slicing disc.

POTATOES: Place them vertically to fill the feed tube. Use a thin slicing disc for potato crisps and game chips. Use a medium or thick slicing disc for potato dishes such as dauphinoise and hot pot toppings.

RADISHES: Place upright in the feed tube, one on top of another and press down lightly with the pusher.

TOMATOES: Use firm, ripe tomatoes and cut in half, if necessary, to fit the feed tube. Use the medium slicing disc.

GRATING DISC

Most food processors have two grating discs which should be sufficient for most processes. You will need a special fine grater for extra hard Parmesan cheese. A very coarse grater of 8 mm or more will double as a french fries cutter or to process root vegetables for stir-frying and salads. Always pre-cut any large pieces of food to fit the feed tube and fill evenly to ensure a good result.

APPLES: Peel, core and quarter. Place one on top of another in the feed tube and press down with the pusher.

CABBAGE: Instead of using the slicing disc a medium or coarse grater can be used to shred cabbage for salads and coleslaw. Trim and remove the hard core. Cut into quarters or eighths to fit the feed tube.

CARROTS: Cut into 6.5 cm (2½ inch) lengths to fit the feed tube horizontally. Neatly stack and press down firmly with the pusher.

CELERIAC: Peel and cut to fit the feed tube.

CHEESE: Cut the cheese to fit the feed tube. Push the cheese carefully. Only suitable for hard cheeses.

CHOCOLATE: Pack upright in the feed tube and press down firmly with the pusher. Use to decorate cakes and desserts.

COURGETTE: Place vertically or horizontally in the feed tube. Use a medium or coarse grating disc.

POTATO: Use raw potatoes only. Use to make rösti potatoes, or a very coarse grating disc for thin french fries.

CHIPPER/STIR-FRY DISC

The chipper, stir-fry and optional julienne discs all produce stick shapes, the size varying according to the aperture size on the disc. As well as producing chipped potatoes it will give sticks of vegetables for stir-frying and salads. Suitable for beetroot, cucumber, celeriac, carrots, courgettes, potatoes, peppers and turnips. Long thin vegetables such as carrots, cucumber and courgettes should be cut into 6.5 cm (2½ inch) lengths and placed horizontally in the feed tube one on top of another, for the best results.

WHISK

This piece of equipment is delicate and should only be used for light mixtures, such as whisking whole eggs, egg whites and double cream. Some manufacturers recommend it for making whisked sponges. Check with your handbook before using.

When whisking egg whites for meringues, soufflés and desserts make sure the food processor bowl is scrupulously clean and free from fat. Use eggs at room temperature and add a little lemon juice or a pinch of salt for a firmer texture. You will see ripples which remain on the surface when the egg whites are stiff. Leave the pusher out of the feed tube to allow the air to circulate in the bowl.

When whipping cream, always use cream which is well chilled. Start on a slow setting if variable speed is available. Take care because it is easy to over-whip cream.

UNSUITABLE FOODS

The food processor takes much of the hard work out of preparing food. However there are a few foods which are not suited to your food processor. Avoid the following:

● Do not use the food processor for crushing or grinding coffee beans.

● Granulated sugar cannot be successfully turned into caster sugar.

● Do not attempt to chop bones, even small ones. Bones are too hard and will irretrievably damage the metal blade.

● Most manufacturers do not advise using the machine to crush ice, because it will blunt he metal blade and may scratch the bowl.

● It cannot grind very hard spices, such as whole nutmeg to a fine powder.

● Very small quantities, of soft tender herbs are not very successful. Either process a larger amount or combine with other ingredients. Parsley, however is the most commonly used herb and can be successfully chopped in very small quantities. Chopping small quantities has been overcome with a number of models by the inclusion of a mini-bowl or multi-mill.

CLEANING

Cleaning the food processor is very easy but essential to ensure safe and hygienic use of the machine.

Always switch off the power supply and remove the plug from the wall socket before cleaning the motor housing. Wipe over the base with a damp cloth and polish with a dry one. Never immerse the motor base in water or pour water over it. Ensure that the safety locking switch and central spindle are clear of any food debris. The food processor bowl, lid, pusher and all the attachments except the whisk may be immersed in water. Depending on the manufacturer, parts of the whisk attachment may not be suitable for immersing in water. Check your handbook for detailed instructions. Immediately after use, rinse the items which have been used in hot soapy water and dry thoroughly. Don't drop the metal blade into a bowl of soapy water. where you can't see it, or you are likely to cut your fingers.

Slicing discs, particularly double sided blades also need to be treated with great care as the cutting edges reach right across the disc, close to the central plastic holder. Also ensure that the cutting edges do not come into contact with hard objects as this might blunt them.

A brush is helpful for cleaning inside the the central spindle hole of the metal blade and dough blade. The inside of the hole may become coated with food when mixing foods which tend to cling. Some food processors include a removable cap on the metal blade and a spatula with prongs, to assist in cleaning the spindle hole.

Most manufacturers state that the blades, discs, bowl, lid and pusher can be washed in the dishwasher.

RECIPE KEY

Each recipe has symbols to represent the food processor attachments used. Check which attachments are needed and assemble them first before you start preparing the recipe.

Metal blade

Dough Blade or Hook

Slicing Disc

Grating Disc

Chipper/Stir-Fry Disc

Whisk

Citrus Press

SOUPS AND STARTERS

Seafood Soup with Rouille

The rich seafood flavour of this soup comes from the home-made stock, using the prawn shells and fresh herbs to enrich a basic fish stock. The food processor makes light work of puréeing the soup and making the rouille.

Preparation time: 20 minutes
Cooking time: 35-40 minutes
Cals per serving: 280
Serves 4

450 g (1 lb) cooked prawns in shell	**salt and pepper**
600 ml (1 pint) fish stock	**ROUILLE**
150 ml (¼ pint) dry white wine	**1 small red chilli**
2 fresh parsley sprigs	**1 garlic clove**
2 bay leaves	**60 ml (4 tbsp) mayonnaise**
4 fresh tarragon sprigs	**30 ml (2 tbsp) low fat fromage frais**
2 medium onions	**TO SERVE**
15 g (½ oz) butter	**8 slices of French bread**
15 g (½ oz) plain white flour	**cayenne pepper**
300 ml (½ pint) milk	

1 Shell the prawns and set aside. Put the prawn shells in a saucepan with the fish stock, wine, parsley, bay leaves and tarragon. Peel the onions and halve one. Add to the saucepan. Bring to the boil, cover and simmer for 20 minutes. Strain the stock through a fine sieve.

2 Fit the metal blade. Quarter and finely chop the remaining onion. Heat the butter in a large saucepan, stir in the onion and sauté gently until softened. Add the flour and cook, stirring, for 1-2 minutes.

3 Gradually pour in the fish stock, stirring constantly, then add the milk. Bring to the boil, stirring, then add the prawns. Simmer gently for 15-20 minutes. Allow to cool slightly, then transfer to the food processor and process in batches until smooth.

4 Meanwhile make the rouille. Halve the chilli and remove the seeds. Peel the garlic. Using the metal blade, place the chilli, garlic, mayonnaise and fromage frais in the food processor and process until smooth.

5 To serve, gently reheat the soup and check the seasoning. Toast the French bread slices on both sides and top with rouille. Divide the soup between warmed serving bowls and float 2 slices of rouille toast on each portion. Serve at once, sprinkled with cayenne and coarsely ground black pepper.

Carrot and Ginger Soup

This tasty carrot soup is topped with a pastry lid. For a lighter soup, omit the pastry topping
and serve the soup topped with a generous spoonful of crème fraîche.

Preparation time: 30 minutes, plus chilling
Cooking time: 45-50 minutes
Cals per serving: 160
Serves 6

275 g (10 oz) onions	**300 ml (½ pint) dry white wine**
900 g (2 lb) carrots	**1.4 litres (2½ pints) vegetable stock**
7.5 cm (3 inch) piece fresh root ginger	**salt and pepper**
2 garlic cloves	**450 g (1 lb) shortcrust pastry**
50 g (2 oz) butter	**beaten egg, to glaze**

1 Peel and quarter the onions. Peel and trim the carrots. Peel the ginger and garlic. Fit the slicing disc and slice the onions, carrots, ginger and garlic.

2 Melt the butter in a large saucepan. Stir in the sliced vegetables and cook, stirring, for 4-5 minutes over a low heat.

3 Add the wine and stock. Bring to the boil, cover and simmer for 20 minutes, or until the vegetables are soft and the flavours are well blended. Cool slightly.

4 Fit the metal blade and process the soup, in batches, until very smooth. Check the seasoning and leave to cool. Fill six ovenproof soup bowls with the cold soup.

5 Roll out the pastry on a lightly floured surface. Lightly dampen the edges of the soup bowls with water. Cut out six strips of pastry 5 mm (¼ inch) wide and press onto the edges of the bowls. Brush the edges with a little egg glaze, then cover the bowls with the remaining pastry. Brush with egg glaze and chill for 15 minutes.

6 Preheat the oven to 230°C (450°F) Mark 8. Bake for 10 minutes, cover with foil and cook for a further 10-15 minutes, until soup is hot and pastry is golden.

Mushroom and Artichoke Soup

Jerusalem artichokes add their own distinctive flavour to this soup. They are cooked in a tasty mushroom stock before puréeing to make a velvety smooth soup. Chopped walnuts add texture to the finished soup.

Preparation time: 20 minutes, plus soaking
Cooking time: 1¼ hours
Cals per serving: 250
Serves 4

15 g (½ oz) dried ceps	**450 g (1 lb) Jerusalem artichokes**
150 ml (¼ pint) boiling water	**1 garlic clove**
1 small onion	**30 ml (2 tbsp) walnut oil**
25 g (1 oz) butter	**salt and pepper**
15 ml (1 tbsp) chopped fresh thyme	**TO SERVE**
450 g (1 lb) chestnut mushrooms	**25g (1 oz) walnuts**
75 ml (3 fl oz) dry sherry	**extra walnut oil**
1.2 litres (2 pints) vegetable stock	**thyme sprigs, to garnish**

1 Put the dried ceps into a bowl, pour over the boiling water and leave to soak for 30 minutes. Drain and reserve the liquid.

2 Fit the metal blade. Peel and quarter the onion, place in the food processor and roughly chop. Melt the butter in a saucepan, add the onion and thyme and fry gently for 10 minutes, until soft but not browned. Using the metal blade, roughly chop the chestnut mushrooms. Add to the saucepan with the ceps and stir-fry for 2 minutes. Add the sherry and boil rapidly until well reduced.

3 Add the vegetable stock and reserved cep stock and bring to the boil. Cover and simmer for 20 minutes until the stock is rich tasting and the mushrooms have lost all their flavour.

4 Meanwhile scrub the artichokes, peel and dice. Peel and chop the garlic. Heat the oil in a large frying pan add the artichokes and garlic and fry for 10 minutes, stirring, until evenly browned.

5 Strain the mushroom liquid through a fine sieve and add to the artichokes. Bring to the boil, cover and simmer for 20-25 minutes until the artichokes are cooked. Transfer to the food processor, fitted with the metal blade and process in batches until smooth.

6 Return the soup to the pan, season to taste and heat gently for 5 minutes. Meanwhile coarsely chop the walnuts, and then lightly toast. Spoon the soup into warmed soup bowls. Scatter the nuts over the top and drizzle with walnut oil. Serve, garnished with thyme.

Spinach and Pea Soup

Spinach and peas are cooked with fresh mint to make this quick and easy soup. After puréeing, the soup is served with a lemon and olive oil dressing which adds a refreshing tang to the soup.

Preparation time: 10 minutes
Cooking time: 30 minutes
Cals per serving: 300
Serves 4

1 medium onion	**900 ml (1½ pints) vegetable or chicken stock**
1 garlic clove	**1.25 ml (¼ tsp) freshly grated nutmeg**
30 ml (2 tbsp) olive oil	**salt and pepper**
2.5 ml (½ tsp) ground cumin	**TO GARNISH**
450 g (1 lb) spinach leaves	**60 ml (4 tbsp) olive oil**
225 g (8 oz) shelled peas (thawed if frozen)	**30 ml (2 tbsp) lemon juice**
4 sprigs fresh mint	**fresh shavings of Pecorino or Parmesan cheese**

1 Fit the metal blade. Peel and quarter the onion. Peel the garlic. Place the onion and garlic in the food processor and roughly chop. Heat the oil in a saucepan, add the onion, garlic and cumin and fry gently for 10 minutes until lightly golden.

2 Wash and dry the spinach leaves and cut away the thick central stalk. Add to the pan with the peas, mint and stock.

3 Bring slowly to the boil, cover and simmer over a very gentle heat for 15 minutes.

4 Transfer to the food processor and blend in batches, until very smooth. Return to the pan and heat gently until the soup reaches the boil. Add the nutmeg and season with salt and pepper.

5 For the garnish, blend together the olive oil and lemon juice. Spoon the soup into warmed serving bowls and drizzle over the lemon oil. Scatter shavings of cheese on top and serve at once.

Chilled Tomato Soup

A quick, refreshing starter, ideal for summer entertaining, which can be made in advance.

Preparation time: 10 minutes, plus chilling

Cooking time: Nil

Cals per serving: 55

Serves 6

1 medium red pepper	60 ml (4 tbsp) Worcestershire sauce
125 g (4 oz) celery	45 ml (3 tbsp) lemon juice
3 garlic cloves	2.5 ml (½ tsp) chilli sauce
small bunch fresh coriander	salt and pepper
900 ml (1½ pints) tomato juice	TO SERVE·
60 ml (4 tbsp) vodka	crushed ice, (optional)

1 Quarter, core and deseed the red pepper. Roughly chop the pepper and celery. Peel the garlic cloves. Fit the metal blade. Place the celery, pepper and garlic in the food processor and finely chop. Add the coriander and process for a few seconds.

2 Mix the tomato juice, vodka, Worcestershire sauce, lemon juice and chilli sauce together. Stir in the chopped vegetables and season with salt and pepper. Cover and chill for at least 1 hour. Serve in individual bowls with a little crushed ice in the centre of each, if desired.

Chilled Beetroot and Apple Soup

A cool, deep crimson soup. Serve with crusty bread or grissini sticks.

Preparation time: 10 minutes, plus chilling

Cooking time: Nil

Cals per serving: 160

Serves 4

350 g (12 oz) cooked, peeled beetroot	salt and pepper
juice of ½ lemon	cayenne pepper
600 ml (1 pint) unsweetened apple juice, chilled	10 cm (4 inch) piece cucumber
200 g (7 oz) Greek-style yogurt, chilled	15 ml (1 tbsp) chopped fresh mint

1 Fit the metal blade. Cut the beetroot into chunks and place in the food processor with the lemon juice, half the apple juice and half the yogurt. Process for 1-2 minutes until smooth. Pass through a sieve into a bowl. Stir in the remaining apple juice, season with salt, pepper and cayenne pepper to taste and chill.

2 Fit the grating disc and grate the cucumber. Stir into the remaining yogurt with the mint. Pour the soup into individual bowls and spoon some cucumber yogurt into the middle of each. Sprinkle with a little cayenne pepper and serve.

Vichyssoise

A variation of this classic soup, it has the added fragrance of oriental lemon grass.
It tastes delicious served well chilled but can also be served hot.

Preparation time: 10 minutes, plus chilling
Cooking time: 35 minutes
Cals per serving: 225
Serves 6

2 medium onions	**300 ml (½ pint) milk**
450 g (1 lb) leeks (white part only)	**salt and pepper**
75 g (3 oz) butter	**150 ml (¼ pint) crème fraîche**
175 g (6 oz) floury potatoes	**TO SERVE**
1 lemon grass stalk	**90 ml (6 tbsp) crème fraîche**
1.3 litres (2¼ pints) vegetable stock	**snipped chives**

1 Peel and quarter the onions. Fit the slicing disc and slice the leeks and onions. Melt the butter in a heavy-based saucepan, add the leeks, onions and 45 ml (3 tbsp) water and stir well. Cover tightly and sweat over a gentle heat for 10 minutes, until soft and lightly golden.

2 Peel the potatoes and slice using the slicing disc. Bruise the lemon grass and add to the pan with the potatoes, stock, milk and seasoning. Bring to the boil, cover and simmer for 20 minutes or until the vegetables are tender.

3 Fit the metal blade. Allow the soup to cool slightly, remove the lemon grass and transfer the soup to the food processor. Blend in batches, until very smooth. Pass through a sieve and stir in the crème fraîche.

4 Chill for 3-4 hours, then taste and adjust the seasoning, if necessary. Serve in individual bowls garnished with a spoonful of crème fraîche and snipped chives.

Grilled Prawns with Spicy Sauce

This tasty tomato, red pepper, chilli and almond sauce is quick to make using the food processor.
It can be served with almost any fish and is delicious both hot and cold.

Preparation time: 15 minutes
Cooking time: 40 minutes
Cals per serving: 315
Serves 4

24 raw king prawns in shell	**2.5 ml (½ tsp) dried chilli flakes**
30-45 ml (2-3 tbsp) olive oil	**75 ml (5 tbsp) fish stock**
SAUCE	**30 ml (2 tbsp) dry white wine**
1 medium onion	**10 blanched almonds**
4 garlic cloves	**15 ml (1 tbsp) red wine vinegar**
1 canned pimiento, drained	**salt**
2 ripe plum tomatoes	**TO GARNISH**
60 ml (4 tbsp) olive oil	**flat-leaf parsley sprigs**

1 To make the sauce, peel the onion and garlic and set one garlic clove aside. Quarter the onion. Fit the metal blade and chop the onion and the remaining garlic cloves.

2 Cut the pimiento into four. Immerse the tomatoes in a bowl of boiling water for 30 seconds, then refresh in cold water. Drain, then peel away the skins. Cut in half and remove the seeds.

3 Heat 30 ml (2 tbsp) of the oil in a pan, add the chopped onion and garlic and cook gently until softened. Using the metal blade, coarsely chop the tomato flesh and pimiento. Add to the saucepan, together with the chilli flakes, fish stock and wine. Cover and simmer for 30 minutes.

4 Preheat the grill and spread the almonds on a baking sheet. Toast the almonds under the grill until golden. Transfer to the cleaned food processor and grind coarsely. Add the remaining oil, vinegar, reserved garlic and salt to taste. Process until evenly combined. Add the tomato sauce and process until smooth.

5 Remove the heads from the prawns and, using a sharp knife, slit each one down the back and remove the black intestinal vein. Rinse in cold water and dry on absorbent kitchen paper.

6 Preheat the grill, toss the prawns in olive oil, then spread out in the grill pan in an even layer. Grill for about 2-3 minutes on each side, until the shells have turned pink. Arrange on a serving platter, garnish with parsley and serve with the sauce.

Carrot and Coriander Roulade

This savoury carrot roulade is filled with a tasty garlic and herb flavoured cream cheese. It could also be served as a light lunch or supper dish.

Preparation time: 30 minutes
Cooking time: 15-20 minutes
Cals per serving: 320-230
Serves 4-6

450 g (1 lb) carrots	**175 g (6 oz) garlic and herb flavoured soft cheese**
50 g (2 oz) butter or margarine	**30 ml (2-3 tbsp) crème fraîche**
small bunch fresh coriander leaves	**TO SERVE**
4 eggs, size 2	**assorted salad leaves and herbs sprigs**
salt and pepper	

1 Preheat the oven to 200°C (400°F) Mark 6. Line a 30 x 20 cm (12 x 8 inch) Swiss roll tin with non-stick baking parchment. Fit the medium or coarse grating disc and grate the carrots.

2 Melt the butter or margarine in a saucepan, add the carrots and cook gently, stirring frequently, for 5 minutes or until slightly coloured. Transfer to a bowl and allow to cool slightly.

3 Using the metal blade, chop the coriander. Reserve 15 ml (1 tbsp) and stir the remainder into the carrots. Separate the eggs, add the egg yolks and beat well. Season with salt and pepper.

4 Using a clean food processor bowl and the whisk attachment, whisk the egg whites until firm peaks form, then stir 30 ml (2 tbsp) into the carrot mix to lighten it. Carefully fold in the rest of the egg whites.

5 Spread the mixture evenly in the prepared tin and bake in the oven for 10-15 minutes until risen and firm to the touch. Turn out onto a sheet of non-stick baking parchment, cover with a clean, damp cloth and allow to cool.

6 Meanwhile, prepare the filling. Using a fork, mix together the soft cheese, reserved coriander and enough crème fraîche to yield a smooth spreading consistency. Adjust the seasoning if necessary.

7 Remove the cloth from the roulade. Spread evenly with the filling, leaving a 1 cm (½ inch) border all round. Carefully roll up from a short side, using the paper to help. To serve, cut into slices and arrange on individual plates with the salad leaves and herbs.

Aubergine Timbales

Thin slices of aubergine are used to line individual moulds which are then filled with a Parmesan and ricotta cheese flavoured with fresh basil. These delicious moulds are served with a red pepper and tomato sauce.

Preparation time: 35 minutes
Cooking time: 20 minutes
Cals per serving: 500

Serves 6

2 aubergines, about 275 g (10 oz) each (preferably short, fat shapes)	**salt and pepper**
90 ml (6 tbsp) olive oil	**25 g (1 oz) fresh basil**
175 g (6 oz) Parmesan cheese	**2 red peppers, about 225 g (8 oz) each**
450g (1 lb) ricotta cheese	**350 g (12 oz) tomatoes**
4 egg yolks	**2 garlic cloves**
5 ml (1 tsp) freshly grated nutmeg	**15 ml (1 tbsp) tomato purée**
	45 ml (3 tbsp) pesto sauce

1 Finely slice the aubergines lengthways. Place on an oiled baking sheet and brush lightly with olive oil. Grill one side until well browned. Set aside.

2 Using the fine or Parmesan grating disc, grate the Parmesan cheese. Fit the metal blade and mix the Parmesan cheese, ricotta cheese, egg yolks, nutmeg and seasoning together. Tear the basil. Reserve 15 ml (1 tbsp) and add the rest to the mixture.

3 Line six 150-175 ml (5-6 fl oz) dariole moulds or ramekins with the aubergine slices, overlapping them with the browned sides facing outwards. Leave a long edge hanging over the outside. Fill each mould with the cheese mixture, pushing it down firmly. Fold the edges of the aubergine over the top of the filling to enclose.

4 Place on a baking sheet and cook at 190°C (375°F) Mark 5 for about 15 minutes or until firm.

5 Meanwhile, make the sauce. Halve and deseed the peppers and tomatoes. Peel the garlic cloves. Using the metal blade, roughly chop the peppers, tomatoes and garlic. Place in a saucepan with the tomato purée and 60 ml (4 tbsp) water and season well. Cook over a gentle heat for 10 minutes. Return to the food processor and process until smooth. Pass through a sieve.

6 Stir in the remaining basil and gently reheat the sauce. To serve, place a pool of sauce on six small plates. Unmould the timbales and place in the centre. Drizzle a little pesto around each timbale and serve.

Fattoush

Fattoush is a flavourful Arabic salad, somewhat reminiscent of a rather solid gazpacho.

Preparation time: 15 minutes, plus chilling
Cooking time: 2-3 minutes
Cals per serving: 185
Serves 4

4 medium tomatoes	**15 ml (3 tbsp) olive oil**
8 sprigs fresh parsley	**salt and pepper**
½ cucumber	**1 pitta bread**
4 spring onions	**TO GARNISH**
1 small green pepper	**roughly torn mint leaves**
1 garlic clove	**black olives**
juice of ½ lemon	

1 Preheat the grill. Put the tomatoes in a heatproof bowl, cover with boiling water and leave for 1 minute. Drain and remove the skins. Fit the metal blade and chop the parsley. Remove and set aside.

2 Roughly chop the tomatoes and cucumber and place in the food processor. Trim and roughly chop the spring onions. Halve, core and deseed the green pepper, then roughly chop the flesh. Peel the garlic.

3 Add the spring onions and green pepper to the food processor with the garlic and lemon juice. Process to a chunky purée.

4 Turn the mixture into a bowl and stir in the chopped parsley, olive oil, salt and pepper.

5 Toast the pitta bread briefly on both sides. Break into small pieces and scatter over the salad.

6 Transfer the salad to one large or four individual serving dishes. Tear the mint leaves over the salad, stud with black olives and serve.

Papaya and Prawn Salad

A light and refreshing starter which is quick to make. The dressing can be made the day before and stored in a cool place until required.

Preparation time: 10-15 minutes

Cooking time: Nil

Cals per serving: 350

Serves 6

2 small red chillies	**30 ml (2 tbsp) runny honey**
30 ml (2 tbsp) white wine vinegar	**salt and pepper**
juice and grated rind of 2 limes	**350 g (12 oz) cooked, peeled king prawns**
150 ml (¼ pint) olive oil	**2-3 ripe papayas**

1 Fit the metal blade. Cut the chillies in half and discard the seeds. Place in the food processor and chop. Add the vinegar, lime juice, olive oil, honey and seasoning. Blend until smooth.

2 Place the dressing in a bowl, and stir in the prawns, coating them thoroughly.

3 Halve and peel the papayas. Scoop out the black seeds and discard. Thinly slice the flesh and arrange on individual serving plates.

4 Carefully spoon the prawn mixture over the papaya slices. Serve immediately, garnished with the grated lime rind. Serve with warm crusty bread.

Celeriac Rémoulade with Trout

This starter includes a recipe for mayonnaise. It is very easy to make in the food processor.
Make double and store the remainder in a clean screw top jar in the refrigerator for 3-4 days.

Preparation time: 20 minutes, plus chilling
Cooking time: 2 minutes
Cals per serving: 270
Serves 6

700 g (1½ lb) celeriac	**RÉMOULADE**
MAYONNAISE	**5 ml (1 tsp) Dijon mustard**
1 egg	**50 g (2 oz) gherkins**
salt and pepper	**30 ml (2 tbsp) capers**
5 ml (1 tsp) mustard powder	**5 sprigs fresh tarragon**
5 ml (1 tsp) lemon juice	**small bunch fresh dill**
200 ml (7 fl oz) olive oil	**175 g (6 oz) sliced smoked trout**
5 ml (1 tsp) white wine vinegar	**TO GARNISH**
	few sprigs of dill

1 Peel the celeriac and cut into 5 cm (2 inch) pieces. Fit the stir-fry disc or chipper disc and cut the celeriac into thin sticks. Place the celeriac in a pan of lightly salted boiling water for 2 minutes, to blanch it. Drain and refresh under cold running water. Drain and set aside.

2 Make the mayonnaise. Fit the metal blade. Place the egg, 2.5 ml (½ tsp) salt, mustard powder and lemon juice in the processor bowl and process for 10 seconds.

3 With the machine running, gradually pour the olive oil down the funnel. Process for 30-60 seconds, until the mixture is thick and creamy. Add the white wine vinegar and process for 20 seconds to mix in.

4 To make the rémoulade, add the Dijon mustard, gherkins, capers, tarragon, dill and seasoning and process for 30 seconds.

5 To serve, mix the rémoulade with the celeriac sticks. Place a 9 cm (3½ inch) round cutter, slightly off centre on a single serving plate, lightly press a little celeriac mixture into the cutter and then carefully remove.

6 Repeat with the remaining mixture on five more serving plates. Arrange the smoked trout beside the celeriac rémoulade and garnish each with a sprig of dill.

Pork and Liver Pâté

Serve this coarse pâté with Melba toast. To make Melba toast, toast slices of crustless bread until golden. Split in half horizontally and toast the cut side, until golden and curled.

Preparation time: 30 minutes, plus chilling
Cooking time: 20 minutes
Cals per serving: 435
Serves 4

50 g (2 oz) piece pancetta or smoked bacon	**pinch of cayenne pepper**
125 g (4 oz) chicken livers	**25 g (1 oz) fresh white bread**
1 small onion	**salt and pepper**
1 garlic clove	**225 g (8 oz) cooked pork**
125 g (4 oz) unsalted butter	**4-6 bay leaves**
5 ml (1 tsp) chopped fresh thyme	**TO SERVE**
60 ml (2½ fl oz) Calvados or brandy	**Melba toast**
2.5 ml (½ tsp) ground mixed spice	

1 Dice the pancetta. Trim and dice the chicken livers. Peel the onion and quarter. Peel the garlic. Fit the metal blade and finely chop the onion and garlic.

2 Heat a heavy-based frying pan, add the pancetta and stir-fry over a high heat until it is browned and has released some fat. Add 25 g (1 oz) butter and fry the onion and garlic for 5 minutes, until golden. Add the chicken livers and thyme and stir-fry for 2 minutes until the livers are browned.

3 Lower the heat and stir in the Calvados or brandy, mixed spice and cayenne. Cover the pan and simmer for 5 minutes. Cool.

4 Cut the bread into large pieces, then process into breadcrumbs. Add the cooled meat mixture and seasoning and process until fairly smooth. Dice and add the pork. Process for a few seconds only, on pulse, to keep the coarse texture of the pork. Spoon into 1 large or 4 small pâté dishes. Smooth the surface.

5 Melt the remaining butter, cool, then pour over the pâté. Leave to cool until the butter is almost set then press in the bay leaves. Chill for several hours or overnight. Serve with Melba toast.

SNACKS AND SUPPERS

Onion Pizza

Pizzas are much quicker to make than you think. The food processor makes the dough in seconds. This pizza is topped with onions, mozzarella and salami. Experiment with your own favourite toppings.

Preparation time: 30 minutes
Cooking time: 45-50 minutes
Cals per serving: 550
Serves 4

175 g (6 oz) strong plain white flour	**60 ml (4 tbsp) olive oil**
2.5 ml (½ tsp) salt	**10 ml (2 tsp) sugar**
5 ml (1 tsp) fast-action dried yeast	**125 g (4 oz) mozzarella cheese**
15 ml (1 tbsp) olive oil	**6 slices salami**
50 g (2 oz) pitted black olives	**10 ml (2 tsp) chopped fresh thyme**
TOPPING	**black pepper**
700 g (1½ lb) onions	

1 Fit the dough blade or hook. Place the flour, salt and yeast in the food processor. With the motor running quickly pour 150 ml (¼ pint) warm water and the olive oil in through the feed tube. Within 15-20 seconds a ball of dough will form. Continue to process for a further 25 seconds.

2 Turn the dough out onto a well-floured surface and knead lightly into a smooth ball. Fit the processor with the metal blade and chop the olives. Knead into the dough. Place in a bowl, cover and leave in a warm place to rise whilst preparing the topping.

3 Fit the slicing disc. Peel the onions and slice. Heat the oil in a frying pan, add the onions and sprinkle with the sugar. Stir well, then cover the pan tightly. Cook gently for about 30 minutes, or until the onions are really soft, but not coloured.

4 Preheat the oven to 220°C (425°F) Mark 7. Roll the dough out into a circle roughly 25 cm (10 inches) in diameter. Place on a lightly greased baking sheet. Place half the onions over the dough.

5 Fit the grating disc and grate the cheese. Sprinkle over the onions. Top with the salami and remaining onion mixture. Sprinkle with thyme and plenty of freshly milled black pepper.

6 Bake for about 20 minutes or until crisp and golden. Serve hot with a crisp green salad.

Courgette and Bacon Frittata

Perfect for a lunchtime snack. Courgettes, onion, bacon and thyme flavour this omelette.
Serve with a tomato and onion salad and warm French bread.

Preparation time: 10 minutes
Cooking time: 10 minutes
Cals per serving: 160
Serves 4

350 g (12 oz) courgettes	**small bunch fresh thyme**
1 medium onion	**3 eggs**
125 g (4 oz) smoked streaky bacon, rindless	**salt and pepper**
15 ml (1 tbsp) sunflower oil	

1 Fit the thick or medium slicing disc and slice the courgettes. Peel and quarter the onion. Fit the metal blade and roughly chop the onion.

2 Roughly chop the bacon. Heat the oil in a 23-25 cm (9-10 inch) frying pan. Sauté the courgettes, onion and bacon together for 4-5 minutes, stirring continuously, until just beginning to soften and turn golden brown.

3 Remove the stalks from the thyme. Using the metal blade chop the herbs. Add the eggs and seasoning and mix together. Pour over the courgette mixture and leave to set over a low heat for 3-4 minutes. Serve immediately, cut into wedges.

Potato and Celeriac Gratin

This recipe relies heavily on the food processor to speed up the preparation. The potatoes, celeriac and onion are quickly sliced into thin slices using the slicing disc.

Preparation time: 10 minutes
Cooking time: 25 minutes
Cals per serving: 545
Serves 4

225 g (8 oz) Gruyère or Gouda cheese	**300 ml (½ pint) single cream**
450 g (1 lb) old potatoes, scrubbed	**1 garlic clove**
450 g (1 lb) celeriac	**125 g (4 oz) finely sliced smoked ham**
1 small onion	**butter, for greasing**
salt and pepper	

1 Fit the grating disc and grate the cheese. Set aside. Fit the slicing-disc and thinly slice the potatoes.

2 Peel and thinly slice the celeriac and onion. Place all the vegetables in a saucepan of lightly salted boiling water and cook for 3-4 minutes, until beginning to soften.

3 Meanwhile place the cream in a saucepan. Peel and crush the garlic, stir into the cream and bring to the boil.

4 Drain the vegetables. Stir into the hot cream with the ham and all but 60 ml (4 tbsp) of the cheese.

5 Season and spoon into a buttered large, shallow, ovenproof dish. Sprinkle with the remaining cheese and cook at 220°C (425°F) Mark 7 for about 20 minutes, or until golden brown.

Mushroom and Stilton Crumble

A satisfying supper dish for meat eaters and vegetarians alike; mushrooms are sautéed in butter then topped with a Stilton cheese sauce and crispy breadcrumbs.

Preparation time: 15 minutes
Cooking time: 25 minutes
Cals per serving: 500-380
Serves 3-4

2 slices brown or white bread	**15 ml (1 tbsp) plain white flour**
25 g (1 oz) walnuts	**225 ml (8 fl oz) milk**
1 small onion	**50 g (2 oz) Stilton cheese**
75 g (3 oz) butter	**salt and pepper**
450 g (1 lb) button mushrooms	**30 ml (2 tbsp) freshly grated Parmesan cheese**

1 Roughly tear the bread into pieces. Fit the metal blade and process the bread and walnuts for 20-30 seconds to make fine crumbs. Remove and set aside.

2 Peel the onion and cut into quarters. Using the metal blade, finely chop the onion. Melt 25 g (1 oz) butter in a frying pan and sauté the onion until soft.

3 Cut any large mushrooms in half. Add all the mushrooms to the pan and cook until brown and any liquid has evaporated.

4 Cut the remaining butter into small cubes and place in the food processor with the flour and milk. Process for about 20 seconds, to blend. Pour into the frying pan and bring to the boil, stirring continuously until thickened.

5 Crumble the Stilton and stir into the mushroom mixture. Season with salt and pepper. Transfer to a 1.1 litre (2 pint) pie dish. Sprinkle the breadcrumb and walnut mixture over the top; finally sprinkle over the Parmesan cheese.

6 Brown under a pre-heated grill for 2-3 minutes, until golden and serve immediately.

Gorgonzola and Rocket Crostini

A speedy pizza style snack, made in minutes. Serve with a mixed green salad.

Preparation time: 15 minutes

Cooking time: 25 minutes

Cals per serving: 510

Serves 4

1 black olive ciabatta	**salt and pepper**
350 g (12 oz) plum tomatoes	**125 g (4 oz) mozzarella cheese**
2 garlic cloves	**175 g (6 oz) Gorgonzola cheese**
30 ml (2 tbsp) sun-dried tomato paste	**25 g (1 oz) fresh rocket**
15 ml (1 tbsp) olive oil	

1 Preheat the oven to 200°C (400°F) Mark 6. Cut the ciabatta in half and then cut horizontally to give 4 pieces. Place on a baking sheet, cut side uppermost. Bake for 5 minutes whilst preparing the filling.

2 Fit the metal blade. Cut the tomatoes in quarters and peel the garlic. Place the tomatoes and garlic in the food processor with the tomato paste, olive oil and salt and pepper. Process for a few seconds until chopped and well blended.

3 Remove the ciabatta from the oven, spread the tomato mixture on top of the bread. Slice the mozzarella and Gorgonzola cheeses thinly and place equal quantities of both on top of each slice of ciabatta. Season with a little black pepper.

4 Bake for 20 minutes, or until the cheese is bubbling. Place a few rocket leaves on top of each slice and serve immediately.

Broccoli Soufflé

Souffles, despite myth, are easy to make. The food processor will blend the sauce ingredients to ensure a smooth sauce.

Preparation time: 15 minutes
Cooking time: 30-35 minutes
Cals per serving: 585

Serves 2

15 ml (1 tbsp) melted butter	**150 ml (5 fl oz) milk**
225 g (8 oz) broccoli	**4 eggs, size 2**
40 g (1½ oz) butter	**25 g (1 oz) freshly grated Parmesan cheese**
40 g (1½ oz) plain white flour	**salt and pepper**

1 Lightly grease a 15 cm (6 inch) soufflé dish with the melted butter. Preheat the oven to 200°C (400°F) Mark 6.

2 Trim the broccoli and cut into florets. Cook in boiling salted water for 2-3 minutes, until just tender. Fit the metal blade. Place the broccoli, butter, flour and milk in the food processor and process for 20-30 seconds until puréed. Pour into a large saucepan and bring to the boil, stirring continuously.

3 Leave the sauce to cool slightly, then separate the eggs and stir in the egg yolks and Parmesan cheese. Season with salt and pepper, to taste.

4 Using a clean food processor bowl and the whisk attachment, whisk the egg whites until stiff. Beat a spoonful into the broccoli mixture to lighten it, then carefully fold in the remainder.

5 Carefully pour the soufflé mixture into the prepared dish and level the top with a palette knife. Stand the dish on a baking sheet. Bake for 25-30 minutes, or until well risen and just set. Serve immediately.

Penne with Olives and Anchovies

This pasta recipe combines penne with a tasty olive, anchovy, garlic and cheese sauce.
Use olives already marinated in flavoured oil, for an even tastier sauce.

Preparation time: 10 minutes
Cooking time: 10 minutes
Cals per serving: 660-440
Serves 4-6

400 g (14 oz) dried penne	**225 g (8 oz) stoned mixed black and green olives**
50 g (2 oz) Parmesan cheese	**60 ml (4 tbsp) olive oil**
8 sprigs fresh parsley	**pepper**
2 garlic cloves	**TO SERVE**
50 g (2 oz) can anchovies in olive oil	**extra Parmesan cheese**
2.5 ml (½ tsp) dried chilli flakes	

1 Bring a large saucepan of salted water to the boil. Add the pasta and cook until 'al dente', or according to the packet instructions.

2 Meanwhile fit the grating disc and grate the cheese. Set aside. Fit the metal blade and chop the parsley. Leave in the food processor.

3 Peel and thinly slice the garlic. Place in a saucepan with the anchovies and their oil. Add the chilli flakes and cook over a fairly high heat for 2-3 minutes, stirring to break up the anchovies with a wooden spoon; do not allow the garlic to brown.

4 Transfer the contents of the pan to the food processor and add the olives and olive oil. Process for a few seconds to give a coarse paste. Season with pepper, to taste.

5 When the pasta is cooked, drain thoroughly in a colander. Return to the saucepan and add the pounded olive mixture and freshly grated Parmesan cheese. Toss well to coat the pasta. Serve immediately, topped with Parmesan shavings.

Spicy Vegetable Parcels

Crisp filo parcels filled with an aromatic rice, parsnip and carrot mixture. Ideal as a light meal or make smaller parcels and serve as a starter.

Preparation time: 20 minutes
Cooking time: 40-45 minutes
Cals per serving: 215
Serves 4

50 g (2 oz) basmati rice	**50 g (2 oz) butter**
225 g (8 oz) parsnips	**small bunch fresh coriander**
125 g (4 oz) carrots	**150 g (5 oz) Greek-style yogurt**
1 small onion	**salt and pepper**
2 garlic cloves	**4 sheets filo pastry each about 28.5 x 50 cm (11 x 19 inches)**
1 small red chilli	
15 ml (1 tbsp) vegetable oil	**10 ml (2 tsp) poppy seeds**
5 ml (1 tsp) garam masala	

1 Cook the rice in a saucepan of boiling salted water, for 12-15 minutes, or until tender. Drain and set aside to cool.

2 Meanwhile, peel the parsnips and carrots. Using the grating disc, grate the parsnips and carrots. Remove and set aside.

3 Peel the onion and garlic. Quarter the onion. Halve and deseed the chilli. Fit the metal blade, add the onion, garlic and chilli and process until finely chopped. Heat the oil in a frying pan, add the onion mixture and sauté together for 5 minutes, or until soft.

4 Stir in the garam masala, grated parsnips and carrots and cook for 3 minutes. Transfer to a large bowl. Melt the butter in a small saucepan. Preheat the oven to 200°C (400°F) Mark 6.

5 Using the metal blade, roughly chop the coriander. Add 30 ml (2 tbsp) to the vegetable mix along with the cooked rice and 30 ml (2 tbsp) yogurt. Stir well to combine and season with salt and pepper.

6 Cut the pastry into eight 23.5 cm (9 inch) squares and brush two with melted butter. Place one on top of the other, to form an 8 point star. Place a quarter of the filling in the centre of the pastry and draw up the edges, pinching the tops together to make little parcels.

7 Repeat with remaining filo pastry and filling. Place the parcels on a greased baking sheet and brush with remaining butter. Sprinkle with poppy seeds. Bake for 15-20 minutes, until golden.

8 Meanwhile stir the remaining coriander and yogurt together and season. Serve with the parcels.

Chicken and Leek Tart

This tart is made with an easy to prepare pastry which is a delight to handle. Use a metal flan tin to cook the tart and the pastry will be crisp without blind baking it first.

Preparation time: 25 minutes
Cooking time: 1 hour
Cals per serving: 615-410
Serves 6-8

PASTRY	25 g (1 oz) butter
225 g (8 oz) plain white flour	**15 ml (1 tbsp) olive oil**
salt and pepper	**275 g (10 oz) cooked chicken**
1 egg	**75 g (3 oz) Gruyère cheese**
45 ml (3 tbsp) olive oil	**150 ml (¼ pint) double or soured cream**
FILLING	**2 eggs**
700 g (1½ lb) trimmed leeks	**freshly grated nutmeg**

1 To make the pastry, put the flour, salt and pepper in the food professor fitted with the metal blade. Process for a few seconds to sift them. Mix the egg, olive oil and 15 ml (3 tbsp) cold water together. Add through the feed tube and process for 20-30 seconds, or until the pastry clings together and forms a ball, adding a little extra water if necessary.

2 Knead the pastry lightly to form a smooth ball then wrap in cling film and leave to rest at room temperature whilst making the filling.

3 Fit the slicing disc. Slit the leeks lengthways and wash thoroughly. Shake dry. Place them vertically in the feed tube and slice the leeks.

4 Heat the butter and oil in a large heavy-based saucepan, add the leeks and cook over a fairly high heat for about 5 minutes. Lower the heat, cover with a tight fitting lid and cook for about 25 minutes, or until really soft. Gently shake the pan from time to time.

5 Roll out the pastry on a lightly floured surface and use to line a shallow 25 cm (10 inch) loose-based flan tin. Cover and chill. Cut the chicken into thin strips. Fit the grating disc and grate the cheese.

6 Preheat the oven to 200°C (400°F) Mark 6. When the leeks are cooked to a soft green mush remove from the heat, and stir in the cheese, cream and eggs. Season with salt, pepper and nutmeg.

7 Arrange the chicken in the pastry case and spoon the leek mixture on top. Bake for about 30 minutes, or until just set in the middle and golden brown. Leave in the tin for 10 minutes, then remove and serve.

Tandoori Pancakes with Raita

Pancake batters are effortlessly made using the food processor. If time allows rest the batter for 30 minutes, before using. Serve with a green salad.

Preparation time: 20 minutes
Cooking time: 10 minutes
Cals per serving: 320
Serves 4

PANCAKE BATTER	1 medium carrot
50 g (2 oz) plain white flour	2 sticks celery
pinch of salt	4 spring onions
1 egg	CUCUMBER RAITA
5 ml (1 tsp) vegetable oil	small bunch fresh coriander
150 ml (¼ pint) milk	5 cm (2 inch) piece cucumber
oil, for frying	150 ml (¼ pint) natural yogurt
FILLING	salt and pepper
350 g (12 oz) cooked tandoori chicken breasts	

1 Make the raita. Fit the metal blade and chop the coriander. Remove and set aside. Fit the grating disc. Cut the cucumber into chunks and feed down the funnel to grate. Remove from the food processor and mix with the yogurt, 30 ml (2 tbsp) chopped coriander and season with salt and pepper.

2 Make the filling. Cut the tandoori chicken into thin strips and place in a bowl. Peel the carrot. Fit the stir-fry disc and cut the celery and carrot into fine strips. Cut the spring onions into 5 cm (2 inch) pieces then into fine strips. Mix all the filling ingredients together with half the cucumber raita.

3 Make the pancake batter. Fit the metal blade. Place the flour, salt, egg, oil, remaining coriander and half the milk in the food processor. Process for 15 seconds to combine. With the machine running add the remaining milk down the feed tube.

4 Lightly oil a frying pan and place over a moderate heat. Add 30 ml (2 tbsp) pancake batter and swirl around to cover the surface. Cook for 1 minute. Turn the pancake using a palette knife and cook for 1 minute. Repeat with remaining mixture to make 8 pancakes.

5 Layer pancakes between sheets of greaseproof paper to prevent them sticking and keep warm. Divide the filling between the pancakes and roll up. Serve with a green salad and the remaining raita.

Pork, Sage and Apple Sausages

Home-made sausages are delicious and using the food processor require little effort. You can always make extra and freeze some for later use.

Preparation time: 20 minutes
Cooking time: 10-15 minutes
Cals per serving: 530-350
Serves 4-6

4 slices brown or white bread	**salt and pepper**
4 sage leaves	**flour, for dusting**
1 small onion	**oil, for frying**
550 g (1¼ lb) belly of pork	**TO SERVE**
1 small eating apple	**crusty bread**
1 egg	**mixed salad leaves**

1 Tear the bread into small pieces, having first removed the crusts. Fit the metal blade and process the bread pieces and sage for 20 seconds, to make fine crumbs. Place in a large bowl.

2 Peel the onion and cut into quarters. Place in the food processor and finely chop. Mix with the breadcrumbs.

3 Trim the meat of skin, connective tissues and any bone. Cut into 2.5 cm (1 inch) chunks. Place in the processor and process for 20-30 seconds, until finely chopped. Add to the breadcrumb mixture.

4 Fit the grating disc. Peel, quarter and core the apple, then grate. Mix into the meat and breadcrumb mixture, with the egg and season generously with salt and pepper. Divide the mixture into 12 pieces.

5 Lightly flour the work surface and roll into 12 sausage shapes. To cook fry in a little oil for 10-15 minutes, until browned and cooked through. If preferred the sausages may be brushed with oil and cooked under a preheated grill. Serve with crusty bread and a mixed leaf salad.

Blue Cheese and Ham Risotto

A wonderfully tasty supper dish. A creamy risotto flavoured with mushrooms, dried ham and dolcelatte cheese.

Preparation time: 15 minutes
Cooking time: 20-25 minutes
Cals per serving: 690
Serves 4

75 g (3 oz) walnuts	1 litre (1¾ pints) vegetable stock
1 medium onion	125 g (4 oz) chestnut mushrooms
1 garlic clove	black pepper
pinch saffron threads	50 g (2 oz) prosciutto or Parma ham
50 g (2 oz) butter	125 g (4 oz) Dolcelatte or Roquefort cheese
350 g (12 oz) Arborio (risotto) rice	TO GARNISH
75 ml (3 fl oz) dry white wine	basil leaves

1 Fit the food processor with the metal blade and coarsely chop the walnuts. Set aside. Peel and quarter the onion and peel the garlic. Place the onion and garlic in the food processor and process for 30 seconds or until chopped. Soak the saffron in 15 ml (1 tbsp) boiling water.

2 Melt the butter in a large heavy-based frying pan, add the onion and garlic and cook for 5 minutes. Stir in the rice and cook for 1 minute. Add the wine and saffron liquid. Cook, stirring occasionally, until the wine is absorbed.

3 Add half the stock, bring to the boil and simmer gently, stirring occasionally, until absorbed for about 10 minutes.

4 Fit the food processor with the slicing disc and slice the mushrooms. Add to the risotto with the remaining stock and cook gently until liquid is absorbed and risotto looks thick and creamy.

5 Stir the walnuts into the risotto and season with pepper, to taste. Tear the ham into thin strips and stir into the rice. Remove from the heat, crumble the cheese over the rice and stir in, until it begins to melt. Sprinkle with basil leaves and serve.

Stir-fried Beef with Chilli

Thin strips of beef are marinated in an aromatic sauce before stir-frying with asparagus, peppers, broccoli and spring onions. Serve on its own as a snack or with rice for supper.

Preparation time: 20 minutes
Cooking time: 15 minutes
Cals per serving: 320
Serves 4

2.5 cm (1 inch) piece fresh root ginger	**450 g (1 lb) rump steak**
1-2 red chillies	**8 asparagus spears**
1 garlic clove	**225 g (8 oz) broccoli**
60 ml (4 tbsp) dark soy sauce	**2 yellow peppers**
30 ml (2 tbsp) mango chutney	**6 large spring onions**
60 ml (4 tbsp) sunflower oil	

1 Fit the metal blade. Peel and halve the ginger, halve and deseed the chillies, peel the garlic. Place in the food processor with the soy sauce and mango chutney and blend until finely chopped. Add half the sunflower oil and blend.

2 Transfer to a dish. Cut the steak into thin strips, add to the dish, toss together and leave to marinate for 30 minutes.

3 Cut the asparagus into 2.5 cm (1 inch) lengths. Divide the broccoli into small florets. Blanch the asparagus and broccoli in boiling water for 2 minutes, then drain thoroughly.

4 Halve and deseed the peppers. Fit the slicing disc and slice the peppers. Place in a bowl. Cut the spring onions in half and slice using the slicing disc.

5 Drain the beef and reserve the marinade. Heat the remaining oil in a large frying or wok, add half the beef and stir-fry for 2-3 minutes. Remove with a slotted spoon and keep warm. Cook the remaining beef and remove as before. Add the broccoli and asparagus and stir-fry for 2 minutes, add the peppers and cook for a further 2 minutes.

6 Return the beef to the pan and reserved marinade. Cook for 2 minutes, then stir in the spring onions and cook for 30 seconds. Transfer to a warmed serving dish, and serve immediately.

FISH AND SHELLFISH

Crispy Cod with Tartare Sauce

These baked cod steaks, finished with a horseradish and herb flavoured crumb topping are served with a crème fraîche based tartare sauce.

Preparation time: 20 minutes
Cooking time: 15-20 minutes
Cals per serving: 210

Serves 6

50 g (2 oz) crustless wholemeal bread	**small bunch fresh dill**
bunch fresh parsley	**6 medium gherkins**
1 lemon	**225 g (8 oz) crème fraîche**
50 g (2 oz) freshly grated horseradish	**TO GARNISH**
salt and pepper	**lemon slices**
6 cod steaks, about 125 g (4 oz) each	**dill sprigs**

1 Preheat the oven to 200°C (400°F) Mark 6. Fit the metal blade. Tear the bread into pieces and process for 20-30 seconds or until medium to fine breadcrumbs are formed. Place in a bowl.

2 Trim the parsley and process until finely chopped. Add 30 ml (2 tbsp) to the breadcrumbs and reserve 30 ml (2 tbsp) for the tartare sauce.

3 Grate the lemon rind and stir into the breadcrumbs with the horseradish and seasoning. Place the cod steaks in a shallow roasting tin and season with salt and pepper.

4 Divide the breadcrumb mixture between the steaks and press on firmly. Bake for 15-20 minutes, or until fish is tender.

5 Meanwhile, prepare the tartare sauce. Chop the dill and gherkins using the metal blade. Stir into the crème fraîche with the reserved parsley. Squeeze the juice from the lemon and flavour the sauce with 10-15 ml (2-3 tsp) to taste. Mix well.

6 Place the cod steaks on warmed serving plates and garnish with lemon slices and dill sprigs. Serve topped with a spoonful of tartare sauce and accompanied by seasonal vegetables.

VARIATIONS

Horseradish sauce can be used if fresh horseradish is unavailable. Spread 10 ml (2 tsp) over each cod steak then top with the flavoured breadcrumb mix.

Braised Cod Boulangère

A perfect supper dish. Layers of potatoes and onion, flavoured with herbs and moistened with stock, topped with thick cod fillets.

Preparation time: 10 minutes

Cooking time: 1 hour

Cals per serving: 395

Serves 4

700 g (1½ lb) potatoes	**300 ml (½ pint) chicken stock**
1 medium onion	**4 thick cod fillets, each about 150 g (5 oz)**
75 g (3 oz) butter	**TO GARNISH**
salt and pepper	**snipped chives**
few fresh thyme sprigs	

1 Preheat the oven to 190°F (375°C) Mark 5. Fit the slicing disc. Peel the potatoes and onion then thinly slice both in the food processor.

2 Use 25 g (1 oz) of the butter to grease an ovenproof dish. Layer the potatoes and onions alternately in the dish, sprinkling each layer with salt, pepper and thyme. Dot with half the remaining butter. Pour in the stock and bake in the oven for 40-50 minutes.

3 Melt the remaining butter in a non-stick frying pan, add the cod fillets and fry briefly until the fish are golden on both sides.

4 Place the fish on top of the potatoes. Cover the dish and return to the oven for a further 10-15 minutes. The fish should be firm, but tender; check by prising the flesh away from the bone - if it comes away evenly, the fish is ready.

5 Sprinkle the fish with the chives and serve immediately with chunks of crusty bread.

VARIATION

Replace the cod fillets with another firm, white fish, such as haddock, whiting or sole.

Smoked Fish Terrine

Smoked haddock and smoked salmon are combined to make this pretty pink and white flecked warm fish mousse.

Preparation time: 20 minutes
Cooking time: 35-40 minutes
Cals per serving: 300-200
Serves 4-6

225 g (8 oz) undyed smoked haddock or cod	**2 egg whites, chilled**
5 ml (1 tsp) finely grated orange rind	**150 ml (¼ pint) whipping cream, chilled**
10 ml (2 tsp) orange juice	**TO SERVE**
freshly ground white pepper	**dill sprigs, to garnish**
225 g (8 oz) smoked salmon	**warm toast**

1 Cut the smoked white fish into chunks and remove any bones. Fit the metal blade. Place the fish in the food processor with the orange rind, orange juice and plenty of pepper. Process until smooth. Cover and chill in the freezer for 10 minutes.

2 Meanwhile roughly chop the smoked salmon. Lightly oil or butter a 900 ml (1½ pint) terrine and line the base with greaseproof paper. Preheat the oven to 180°C (350°F) Mark 4.

3 Remove the processor bowl from the freezer and place on the machine again. With the machine running, add the egg whites through the feeder tube, then the cream; do not overwork or the mixture will curdle. Turn out into a bowl. Gently stir in the smoked salmon so the mixture is flecked with pink.

4 Carefully fill the terrine with the mixture, packing it down well to exclude trapped pockets of air, then level the surface. Cover the terrine with buttered greaseproof paper.

5 Stand the terrine in a roasting tin and pour in enough boiling water to come halfway up the side. Bake in the preheated oven for 35-40 minutes, or until firm to the touch.

6 Run a thin-bladed knife around the terrine and unmould onto a warmed platter. Cut into slices and arrange on individual plates. Garnish with dill and serve warm with toast.

Thai Fish Cakes

These fish cakes bear no resemblance to British fish cakes. They are flavoured with chilli, lime and coriander. Serve with a crunchy salad of bean sprouts and shredded cabbage, tossed in a soy sauce based dressing.

Preparation time: 25 minutes
Cooking time: 20 minutes
Cals per serving: 250
Serves 4

small bunch fresh coriander leaves	**flour, for coating**
450 g (1 lb) white fish fillets	**oil, for shallow frying**
4 kaffir lime leaves	**TO SERVE**
15 ml (1 tbsp) nam pla (Thai fish sauce)	**salad leaves**
15 ml (1 tbsp) lime juice	**shredded spring onions**
30 ml (2 tbsp) Thai red curry paste	**lime halves**
salt and pepper	

1 Fit the metal blade. Chop the coriander and set aside. Remove any skin from the fish, then place in the food processor and process until smooth.

2 Finely chop the lime leaves and add to the fish with the coriander, nam pla, lime juice and red curry paste. Season with salt and pepper and process until thoroughly mixed.

3 Using lightly floured hands, divide the mixture into 12 pieces and shape each one into a small cake, about 5 cm (2 inches) in diameter.

4 Shallow fry the fish cakes in batches. Heat a 1 cm (½ inch) depth of oil in a frying pan. Cook the fish cakes, a few at a time, for about 4 minutes each side. Drain on absorbent kitchen paper and keep hot whilst cooking the remainder.

5 Serve the fish cakes as soon as they are all cooked, on a bed of salad leaves, scattered with shredded spring onions. Serve with lime halves.

NOTE: Thai red curry paste is available in jars from large supermarkets and delicatessens.

Curried Fish with Ginger

Fillets of sole in a creamy coconut and ginger sauce. Serve with basmati rice and chapatis or naan bread.

Preparation time: 20 minutes, plus marinating
Cooking time: 20-25 minutes
Cals per serving: 275

Serves 6

5 cm (2 inch) piece fresh root ginger	**finely grated rind and juice 1 lemon**
2 garlic cloves	**salt and pepper**
5 ml (1 tsp) garam masala	**50 g (2 oz) creamed coconut**
12 sole fillets, skinned, about 1.1 kg (2½ lb) total weight	**2.5 ml (½ tsp) saffron threads**
small bunch fresh coriander	**25 g (1 oz) salted cashew nuts**
175 g (6 oz) spring onions	**15 ml (1 tbsp) oil**
	150 ml (¼ pint) single cream

1 Peel and finely chop the ginger. Peel and crush the garlic. Mix the ginger, garlic and garam masala together. Place the sole fillets in a flat non-metallic dish and rub with the spice mixture. Cover tightly and leave to marinate in the refrigerator overnight.

2 Fit the metal blade. Add the coriander and process for a few seconds until finely chopped. Remove and set aside. Add the spring onions and roughly chop. Mix half the spring onions with 30 ml (2 tbsp) chopped coriander, lemon rind and 45 ml (3 tbsp) lemon juice and seasoning.

3 Place the fillets, skinned side up, on a plate and spoon a little of the onion mixture into the centre of each. Roll up and secure with a wooden cocktail stick.

4 Put the creamed coconut, saffron and cashew nuts in the food processor with 200 ml (7 fl oz) water and process until smooth.

5 Heat the oil in a large shallow flameproof casserole and sauté the remaining spring onions for 2-3 minutes. Add the coconut liquid and any remaining marinade. Bring to the boil and cover. Simmer very gently, for 15 minutes, or until the fish is tender.

6 Add the cream and heat gently without boiling for a further 2-3 minutes. Adjust the seasoning. Remove the cocktail sticks and serve garnished with the remaining chopped coriander.

Filo Wrapped Oriental Sole

Sole fillets are wrapped around a ginger, dill and prawn stuffing. Each sole fillet is wrapped in filo pastry to make a delicate purse which is served on a pool of ginger butter sauce.

Preparation time: 35 minutes
Cooking time: 20-25 minutes
Cals per serving: 735

Serves 4

3 spring onions	**GINGER SAUCE**
2.5 cm (1 inch) piece fresh root ginger	**1 shallot**
225 g (8 oz) peeled prawns	**4 thin slices fresh root ginger**
small bunch fresh dill	**75 ml (5 tbsp) white wine vinegar**
1 egg white	**175 g (6 oz) unsalted butter**
45 ml (3 tbsp) whipping cream	**2 egg yolks**
salt and pepper	**squeeze of lemon juice**
4 double sole fillets	**TO GARNISH**
75 g (3 oz) butter	**shredded spring onion**
8 sheets filo pastry	

1 Cut the onions in half. Peel the ginger and cut in half. Fit the metal blade and chop the onions and ginger. Add the prawns and dill and process to a paste. Add the egg white, cream and seasoning. Process to combine.

2 Cut the sole fillets in half and spread evenly with the prawn paste. Roll up from the thick end and secure with a cocktail stick. Place in a shallow pan. Add 150 ml (¼ pint) water and slowly bring to a bare simmer. Cover tightly and turn off the heat. Leave to partially cook in the residual heat for 10 minutes. Remove, drain and cool.

3 Melt the butter. Cut each sheet of filo pastry into 2 x 18-20 cm (7-8 inch) squares and cover with a damp tea towel. Brush two squares with melted butter and place one on top of the other to form an 8 point star.

4 Place a fish roll in the middle and draw the filo up and around the fish, twisting to secure. Frill out the top and place the filo purse on a baking sheet. Repeat with remaining fish and filo pastry. Drizzle with butter and bake for 10-15 minutes, until golden.

5 Meanwhile peel and chop the shallot. Place in a small pan with the ginger and vinegar and boil until reduced to 45 ml (3 tbsp). Discard the ginger. Melt the butter. Fit the metal blade, add the egg yolks, switch on and through the feed tube slowly add the vinegar and then the butter. Stop when emulsified and thickened. Stir in the lemon juice and season to taste.

6 Arrange two purses on each warmed plate on a pool of sauce. Sprinkle with spring onion and serve.

Roasted Monkfish with Pesto

This roasted monkfish stuffed with rocket pesto is full of flavour and wonderfully succulent. It is roasted on a bed of shallots and garlic. Serve with boiled new potatoes or rice and steamed mangetouts.

Preparation time: 30 minutes
Cooking time: 40-45 minutes
Cals per serving: 320

Serves 4

225 g (8 oz) shallots	**4 fresh thyme sprigs**
4 garlic cloves	**4 fresh oregano sprigs**
30 ml (2 tbsp) cider vinegar	**ROCKET PESTO**
30 ml (2 tbsp) olive oil	**50 g (2 oz) rocket leaves**
900 g (2 lb) monkfish tails (on the bone)	**25 g (1 oz) fresh Parmesan cheese**
salt and pepper	**15 ml (1 tbsp) olive oil**
4 fresh rosemary sprigs	**30 ml (2 tbsp) apple juice**

1 Preheat the oven to 220°F (425°C) Mark 7. Peel the shallots and cut in half. Place in a roasting pan with the garlic, sprinkle with cider vinegar and oil and cook for 20 minutes.

2 Meanwhile make the pesto. Wash the rocket leaves. Fit the grating disc and grate the Parmesan cheese. Fit the metal blade and place the rocket and olive oil in the food processor with the cheese. With the machine running pour the apple juice through the feeder tube in a steady stream. Blend until a smooth paste is formed.

3 Remove any skin and membrane from the monkfish: cut around the membrane, pull back and tear off using your fingers. Cut along one side of the centre bone, as close to the bone as possible and remove the fillet. Repeat on the other side.

4 Lay one fillet, cut side up, on a board and spread with the pesto. Place the other fillet on top, cut side down, to sandwich the pesto. Tie the two pieces together at regular intervals with string.

5 Remove the roasting pan from the oven, push the shallots and garlic to the sides, and lay the monkfish parcel in the centre of the pan. Sprinkle with salt and pepper and add the herb sprigs. Cook for 20-25 minutes, until the monkfish turns opaque.

6 To serve, remove the string and lift the monkfish on to a serving platter, discarding any milky residue. Place the shallots and garlic around the fish.

Roast Salmon with Peanut Crust

A piquant crunchy topping, transforms simple salmon steaks into a special dish. The peanut and breadcrumb topping can be made in advance. Serve with a mixed leaf salad and new potatoes.

Preparation time: 10 minutes
Cooking time: 15-20 minutes
Cals per serving: 800
Serves 4

75g (3 oz) crustless white bread	**small bunch fresh parsley**
3-4 spring onions	**175 g (6 oz) unsalted butter, softened**
75 g (3 oz) salted roasted peanuts	**finely grated rind of ½ lemon**
1 red chilli	**salt and pepper**
2.5 cm (1 inch) piece fresh root ginger	**4 salmon fillets, about 175 g (6 oz) each**

1 Fit the metal blade. Cut the bread into large pieces and process to make breadcrumbs. Remove and set aside. Cut the spring onions into four, then place in the food processor with the peanuts and roughly chop. Remove and set aside.

2 Cut the chilli in half and remove the seeds. Peel the ginger and cut in half. Place the parsley in the food processor and process for a few seconds until finely chopped. Add the chilli and ginger and process until finely chopped. Add the butter and lemon rind and blend together.

3 Put 50 g (2 oz) of the flavoured butter in a frying pan and heat gently to melt. Add the breadcrumbs, spring onions and peanuts and fry, until golden, stirring continuously to prevent the breadcrumbs from sticking. Season with salt and pepper.

4 Preheat the oven to 200°C (400°F) Mark 6. Arrange the salmon fillets, skin side uppermost, in a roasting tin. Spoon the fried breadcrumb mix on top. Cook for 10-15 minutes, or until the salmon is just cooked.

5 Melt the remaining flavoured butter, arrange the salmon steaks on warmed serving plates and drizzle over the melted butter.

Tuna and Celeriac Salad

Finely shredded and lightly cooked, celeriac makes a delicious base for this refreshing salad. Both the salad and dressing can be made in advance, but don't add the rocket until just before serving.

Preparation time: 15 minutes
Cooking time: 2 minutes
Cals per serving: 260
Serves 4

	DRESSING
700 g (1½ lb) celeriac	**150 ml (¼ pint) soured cream**
salt and pepper	**30 ml (2 tbsp) mayonnaise**
200 g (7 oz) can tuna in oil	**15 ml (1 tbsp) wholegrain mustard**
30 ml (2 tbsp) capers	**small bunch fresh chives**
finely grated rind of 1 lemon	**6 sprigs fresh parsley**
50 g (2 oz) rocket or watercress	**salt and pepper**

1 Cut the skin off the celeriac. Cut the celeriac into pieces thin enough to fit in the feed tube.

2 Using the slicing disc, slice the celeriac. Remove from the bowl and slice again to shred into small pieces.

3 Bring a large saucepan of lightly salted water to the boil. Add the celeriac and boil for 2 minutes, until just softened, but still retaining a little texture. Drain and refresh in cold water. Drain thoroughly and place in a large bowl.

4 Drain the tuna and add to the bowl with the capers, salt and pepper and lemon rind.

5 Make the dressing. Fit the cleaned food processor with the metal blade. Add the soured cream, mayonnaise, mustard and herbs and blend until the herbs are finely chopped and colour the dressing.

6 Lightly toss the rocket or watercress with the salad. Pour over the dressing and serve.

Pink Trout with Almonds

A purée of toasted almonds, garlic, parsley and Parmesan cheese complements the delicate flavour of the trout. The fresh pink trout is basted with a lemon and paprika butter and grilled until crisp.

Preparation time: 20 minutes
Cooking time: About 15 minutes
Cals per serving: 745

Serves 4

4 pink-fleshed trout, each about 275 g (10 oz), cleaned	**30 ml (2 tbsp) freshly grated Parmesan cheese**
50 g (2 oz) butter	**50 g (2 oz) fresh parsley sprigs**
15 ml (1 tbsp) lemon juice	**150 ml (¼ pint) light olive oil**
10 ml (2 tsp) paprika	**30 ml (2 tbsp) fromage frais**
75 g (3 oz) blanched whole almonds	**salt and pepper**
1 garlic clove	**to garnish**
	parsley sprigs

1 Preheat the grill. Rinse the trout and pat dry with absorbent kitchen paper.

2 Place the butter, lemon juice and paprika in a saucepan over a low heat until the butter melts. With a sharp knife, make diagonal slashes on both sides of each trout. Lay the trout in a foil-lined grill pan and brush with the paprika butter.

3 Spread the almonds on a baking sheet and place under the grill for 2-3 minutes, turning frequently until toasted and golden.

4 Fit the metal blade. Place 50 g (2 oz) of the toasted almonds in the food processor. Peel the garlic. Add to the food processor with the Parmesan cheese, parsley, olive oil, fromage frais and salt and pepper. Blend until smooth. Roughly chop the remaining almonds and set aside.

5 Grill the trout for 5-7 minutes on each side, or until opaque and cooked through, basting from time to time with the paprika butter.

6 Transfer the trout to warmed serving plates. Spoon a portion of toasted almond and herb purée onto each plate and scatter over the remaining toasted almonds. Garnish with sprigs of parsley and serve immediately.

Scallops with Pepper Purée

A superb pasta dish using thick ribbon pasta. The pasta is tossed with scallops and a grilled pepper purée sauce.

Preparation time: 20 minutes
Cooking time: 35 minutes
Cals per serving: 780-520
Serves 4-6

4 red peppers	**small bunch fresh parsley**
6 garlic cloves	**50 g (2 oz) Parmesan cheese**
450 g (1 lb) medium scallops	**400 g (14 oz) dried ribbon pasta, such as tagliatelle or pappardelle**
75 ml (5 tbsp) extra-virgin olive oil	
5 ml (1 tsp) paprika	**15 ml (1 tbsp) balsamic vinegar or lemon juice**
coarse sea salt and pepper	

1 Preheat the grill to hot. Place the whole peppers and unpeeled garlic cloves on the grill rack and grill, turning from time to time, until the peppers are blackened and blistered all over. This will take about 20 minutes, by which time the garlic cloves will be soft and tender. Allow to cool slightly.

2 Holding them over a bowl to catch the juices, peel the peppers, then remove the core and seeds. Peel the garlic. Chop the peppers roughly. Fit the metal blade and place the peppers and garlic in the food processor. Process for a few seconds to give a coarse purée.

3 Thread the scallops onto wooden skewers. Line the grill pan with foil to catch the juices. Brush the scallops with 30 ml (2 tbsp) of the olive oil and sprinkle with paprika. Season liberally with sea salt and pepper. Grill for 4-5 minutes, turning once halfway through cooking, until just firm. Remove the scallops from their skewers, and slice if large.

4 Using the metal blade chop the parsley and set aside. Fit the fine grating disc and grate the Parmesan cheese. Cook the pasta in a large pan of boiling salted water until 'al dente', or according to the pack instructions.

5 Meanwhile, transfer the pepper purée to a large frying pan. Heat gently, then stir in the scallops and the juices from the grill pan. Cook over a gentle heat for 1 minute, then stir in the parsley and balsamic vinegar or lemon juice. Remove from the heat.

6 Drain the pasta thoroughly in a colander and return to the pan. Add the remaining 45 ml (3 tbsp) olive oil and toss to mix. Add the scallops in pepper sauce and toss again lightly. Serve at once sprinkled with the Parmesan cheese.

Garlic Stuffed Mussels

Cooked mussels, mixed with leeks and cream, coated in garlic breadcrumbs, make a lovely starter or light meal with salad. If available use large mussels as they will be less fiddly to prepare.

Preparation time: 20 minutes
Cooking time: 10 minutes
Cals per serving: 155
Serves 4

450 g (1 lb) large mussels	**freshly grated nutmeg**
45 ml (3 tbsp) dry white wine	**25 g (1 oz) butter**
4 sprigs fresh parsley	**1 garlic clove**
salt and pepper	**TO GARNISH**
50 g (2 oz) leek, green end only	**flat-leaf parsley sprigs**
25 g (1 oz) crustless white bread	**lemon wedges**
45 ml (3 tbsp) double cream	

1 Scrub the mussels, discarding any which are damaged or open ones which do not close when tapped with a knife.

2 Put the wine, parsley and a little salt and pepper in a large saucepan and bring to the boil. Add the mussels, cover with the lid and cook for 3-4 minutes, or until mussels have opened.

3 Cool slightly, then remove the mussels from their shells, splitting each shell and reserving half. Bring a little water to the boil in a small saucepan, add the leek and cook for 1 minute. Drain and cut into quarters.

4 Fit the metal blade. Break the bread into pieces and process into breadcrumbs. Set aside. Place the mussels and leeks in the food processor and process until finely chopped. Stir in the cream, a little nutmeg and season to taste.

5 Arrange the reserved shell halves on a baking sheet and spoon the mussel mixture into the shells. Melt the butter. Peel and crush the garlic and mix with the melted butter and prepared breadcrumbs.

6 Heat the grill to moderate. Spoon the breadcrumb mixture over the mussels and grill lightly until golden. Serve immediately, garnished with parsley and lemon.

Choux Buns with Crab

Choux pastry is much easier to make in the food processor and puffs up beautifully when baked.
The little buns are filled with a fresh crab meat, mayonnaise and chive filling.

Preparation time: 20 minutes, plus cooling
Cooking time: 25-30 minutes
Cals per serving: 435
Serves 4

CHOUX PASTRY	175 g (6 oz) fresh dressed crab
65 g (2½ oz) plain white flour	90 ml (6 tbsp) mayonnaise
50 g (2 oz) butter	dash of Tabasco sauce
2 eggs	TO SERVE
15 ml (1 tbsp) ground almonds	flat-leaf parsley sprigs
2.5 ml (½ tsp) paprika	mixed leaf salad
FILLING	
45 ml (3 tbsp) snipped fresh chives	

1 Preheat the oven to 220°C (425°F) Mark 7. Lightly grease and dampen a baking sheet. Sift the flour.

2 Put the butter and 150 ml (¼ pint) water into a small saucepan. Heat gently until the butter has melted, then bring to the boil. Remove from the heat and tip in the flour. Beat with a wooden spoon until combined.

3 Return the pan to the heat and cook over a low heat until the mixture forms a ball which comes away from the sides of the pan.

4 Fit the food processor with the metal blade and add the flour paste. Beat the eggs together. Turn the food processor on and slowly pour the eggs through the feeder tube. Process until the mixture forms a stiff, glossy paste.

5 Place teaspoonfuls onto the prepared baking sheet. Mix together the ground almonds and paprika and sprinkle over the pastry. Bake for 20-25 minutes until well risen and golden.

6 Reduce the oven to 180°C (350°F) Mark 4. Make a slit in the side of each bun, then return to the oven for 5 minutes, to dry out completely. Cool on a wire rack.

7 Mix the chives, crab, mayonnaise and Tabasco together. Spoon a little filling into each bun. Garnish with parsley and serve with a mixed leaf salad.

MEAT AND POULTRY

Beef and Mushroom Casserole

Dark, rich and wonderfully tasty, this winter stew is delicious served with mashed or jacket potatoes.

Preparation time: 20 minutes

Cooking time: 2¼ hours

Cals per serving: 305

Serves 6

225 g (8 oz) shallots	300 ml (½ pint) beef stock
50 g (2 oz) butter	440 ml can Guinness
15 g (½ oz) dried wild mushrooms	salt and pepper
900 g (2 lb) stewing steak	225 g (8 oz) carrots
45 ml (3 tbsp) plain white flour	225 g (8 oz) celeriac

1 Peel the shallots. Fit the slicing disc and feed the shallots down the feed tube to slice. Melt 25 g (1 oz) butter in a frying pan and sauté the shallots until soft. Transfer to an ovenproof casserole.

2 Soak the dried mushrooms in 150 ml (¼ pint) boiling water and set aside.

3 Cut the stewing steak into 5 cm (2 inch) chunks and sauté in batches until brown. Add to the shallots. Preheat the oven to 180°C (350°F) Mark 4.

4 Fit the metal blade. Place the remaining butter, flour and stock in the food processor bowl and process for 20 seconds. Pour into the frying pan and add the Guinness.

5 Bring to the boil and cook for 2 minutes, stirring continuously. Pour into the casserole and season. Add the mushrooms and their soaking liquid. Cover the casserole tightly and cook in the oven for 1½ hours.

6 Peel the carrots and celeriac and cut into 5 cm (2 inch) chunks. Fit the stir-fry or chipper disc and cut into thin sticks. Add to the casserole and cook for a further 30 minutes or until meat and vegetables are tender. Serve with mashed potato or crusty bread.

Country Pie

A hearty meal on it's own. Minced beef, onions, carrots and parsnips are covered with potato slices and then with soured cream and Cheddar cheese, which bakes to a golden brown topping. Serve with a green vegetable.

Preparation time: 15 minutes
Cooking time: 1¼-1½ hours
Cals per serving: 480
Serves 6

1 large onion	700 g (1½ lb) minced beef
1 garlic clove	60 ml (4 tbsp) sun-dried tomato paste
15 ml (1 tbsp) vegetable oil	30 ml (2 tbsp) brandy
50 g (2 oz) Cheddar cheese	salt and pepper
125 g (4 oz) carrots	800 g (1¾ lb) medium potatoes
125 g (4 oz) parsnips	300 ml (½ pint) soured cream

1 Peel the onion and cut into quarters. Peel the garlic. Fit the metal blade, add the onion and garlic and process until finely chopped. Heat the oil in a frying pan add the onion and garlic and cook for 10 minutes until soft. Remove from the heat and set aside.

2 Meanwhile fit the grating disc. Grate the Cheddar cheese and set aside. Peel the carrots and parsnips and grate.

3 Add the minced beef to the frying pan and sauté until brown. Return the onions to the pan. Add the carrots, parsnips, sun-dried tomato paste, brandy and salt and pepper and cook for 5 minutes, stirring occasionally.

4 Preheat the oven to 180°C (350°F) Mark 4. Scrub the potatoes and cut to fit the feed tube. Fit the thick slicing disc and slice the potatoes.

5 Pour the meat mixture into a 2.3 litre (4 pint) round ovenproof dish. Arrange the potato slices overlapping to cover the surface. Spread the soured cream over the top and sprinkle with the grated cheese.

6 Place on a baking sheet and bake for 1-1¼ hours until golden brown and the potatoes are tender.

Beef Fillet with Walnut Topping

A very easy dish, which can be prepared in advance. A tasty walnut and garlic mixture tops the juicy fillet steaks which cook in the oven in minutes.

Preparation time: 30 minutes
Cooking time: 15-20 minutes
Cals per serving: 680
Serves 6

225 g (8 oz) walnut pieces	30 ml (2 tbsp) sunflower oil
125 g (4 oz) pickled walnuts, drained	60 ml (4 tbsp) dry red wine
2 garlic cloves	15 ml (1 tbsp) tomato purée
30 ml (2 tbsp) thick soy sauce	300 ml (½ pint) well-flavoured beef stock
45 ml (3 tbsp) olive oil	**TO SERVE**
salt and pepper	4 large radicchio leaves (optional)
1-1.1 kg (2¼-2½ lb) piece fillet of beef, trimmed	parsley sprigs

1 Roughly chop both types of walnut together and set aside one half. Peel the garlic. Fit the metal blade and add half of the chopped nuts to the food processor with the garlic, soy sauce and olive oil. Blend until smooth. Stir in the reserved walnuts and season with salt and pepper. The paste should be quite thick and lumpy.

2 Slice the fillet into six thick steaks. Heat the oil in a heavy-based frying pan until almost smoking. Fry the steaks, one at a time, very quickly on all sides to brown and seal. Allow to cool. Top each steak thickly with the walnut paste. Cover and refrigerate until ready to cook.

3 To make the gravy, deglaze the frying pan with the wine, stirring to scrape up the sediment. Add the tomato purée and beef stock, bring to the boil and boil steadily for 2-3 minutes until reduced slightly. Check the seasoning. Pour into a bowl and cool. Cover and refrigerate until needed.

4 Remove the steaks from the refrigerator 15-20 minutes before cooking to allow them to come to room temperature. Preheat the oven to 200°C (400°F) Mark 6.

5 Place the steaks on a baking sheet. Bake in the oven for 10-15 minutes, depending on thickness and preference for rare or medium cooked steaks. Meanwhile reheat the gravy in a small pan.

6 Serve the steaks on warmed serving plates as soon as they are cooked. If desired, place each one on a radicchio leaf and garnish with parsley sprigs. Serve with the gravy.

NOTE: Pickled walnuts are available in jars from large supermarkets and delicatessens. If unobtainable, simply increase the quantity of fresh walnut pieces by 125 g (4 oz) and add 15 ml (1 tbsp) wine vinegar to the food processor.

Sautéed Liver with Capers

Excellent for entertaining, tender sweet calf's liver needs only the briefest cooking. Serve with new potatoes and crisp young sugar snap peas.

Preparation time: 15 minutes
Cooking time: 15 minutes
Cals per serving: 350
Serves 4

125 g (4 oz) shallots	**150 ml (¼ pint) chicken stock**
50 g (2 oz) butter	**60 ml (4 tbsp) crème fraîche**
450 g (1 lb) thinly sliced calf's liver	**30 ml (2 tbsp) capers**
15 ml (1 tbsp) plain white flour	**30 ml (2 tbsp) chopped fresh chervil**
15 ml (1 tbsp) lemon juice	**salt and pepper**

1 Peel the shallots. Fit the slicing disc and slice. Heat 25 g (1 oz) butter in a frying pan until foaming. Sauté the liver for 2 minutes on each side. Remove and keep warm. Add the shallots to the pan and sauté until soft.

2 Meanwhile fit the metal blade and add the remaining butter, flour, lemon juice and chicken stock. Process for 20 seconds or until blended. Pour into the frying pan with the shallots and bring to the boil, stirring continuously until thickened.

3 Reduce the heat and stir in the crème fraîche, capers and chervil. Season to taste with salt and pepper. Heat through, but do not boil.

4 Arrange the calf's liver on warmed serving plates and pour a little sauce over each. Serve immediately.

Stuffed Shoulder of Lamb

Roast lamb is always a firm favourite. Boned shoulders of lamb are available in most supermarkets, or ask your butcher to prepare the meat for you.

Preparation time: 20 minutes
Cooking time: 1¾ hours
Cals per serving: 600
Serves 6

2 large crustless slices white bread	**225 g (8 oz) onion**
few sprigs fresh thyme	**50 g (2 oz) butter**
few sprigs fresh parsley	**1.25 ml (¼ tsp) ground nutmeg**
50 g (2 oz) shelled pistachio nuts	**salt and freshly ground black pepper**
175 g (6 oz) ready soaked pitted prunes	**1.4 kg (3 lb) boned shoulder or leg of lamb**
50 g (2 oz) ready soaked dried apricots	**150 ml (¼ pint) red wine**

1 Fit the metal blade. Tear the bread into large pieces. Place in the food processor with the leaves from the thyme and parsley and the pistachio nuts. Process for 1 minute, or until finely chopped. Transfer to a bowl.

2 Put 50 g (2 oz) prunes and the apricots in the food processor and finely chop. Stir into the crumb mixture.

3 Peel the onion and quarter. Place in the food processor and finely chop. Melt the butter in a small saucepan and sauté the onion until soft and transparent, stirring occasionally. Stir into the crumb mixture with the nutmeg and season with salt and pepper. Mix well and leave to cool.

4 Preheat the oven to 200°C (400°F) Mark 6. Unroll the shoulder of lamb, spoon the filling into the lamb, roll up again and tie at regular intervals — don't worry if a little of the stuffing begins to ooze out.

5 Place the lamb in a dry roasting tin and cook for about 1½ hours, basting occasionally. Test with a fine skewer. If the meat juices are pink, the lamb is slightly underdone. Cook for a little longer if you prefer it well done. Place the lamb on a heated serving dish, cover and keep warm.

6 Drain off most of the fat from the roasting tin, then add the wine with 300 ml (½ pint) water. Bring to the boil, scraping all the sediment off the base of the pan. Strain into a small saucepan. Add the reserved prunes and simmer for about 5 minutes. Adjust the seasoning and serve with the sliced lamb.

Lamb Meatballs with Dill Sauce

Cinnamon adds a delicate hint of spice to these meatballs which are served with a creamy white wine and dill sauce.

Preparation time: 30 minutes
Cooking time: 1 hour 10 minutes
Cals per serving: 650
Serves 6

6 spring onions	**450 ml (¾ pint) dry white wine**
175 g (6 oz) unsmoked streaky bacon	**bunch of fresh dill**
1 garlic clove	**300 ml (½ pint) double cream**
pinch of ground cinnamon	**2 egg yolks**
700 g (1½ lb) lean minced lamb	**TO GARNISH**
salt and pepper	**dill sprigs**
45 ml (3 tbsp) olive oil	**lemon wedges**

1 Fit the metal blade. Trim the spring onions, roughly chop the bacon and peel the garlic. Place the spring onions, bacon, garlic and cinnamon in the food processor and blend until almost smooth. Add the minced lamb and plenty of salt and pepper. Process until well mixed and smooth.

2 With wet hands, shape the mixture into 30-36 even sized balls. Keep wetting your hands to prevent it sticking.

3 Preheat oven to 180°C (350°F) Mark 4. Heat the oil in a large frying pan and brown the meatballs in batches, then transfer to a shallow ovenproof dish.

4 Pour the wine into the frying pan and bring to the boil, scraping any sediment from the bottom of the pan. Pour over the meatballs, cover and bake for 1 hour.

5 Finely chop the dill using the metal blade. Pour the cooking liquid into a saucepan. Cover the meatballs and keep warm. Bring the liquid to the boil and boil rapidly until reduced to 300 ml (½ pint).

6 Lower the heat and stir in 60 ml (4 tbsp) chopped dill, cream and egg yolks. Stir over a gentle heat for about 10 minutes, or until slightly thickened; do not allow to boil. Taste and adjust the seasoning.

7 Transfer the meatballs to warmed serving plates and spoon the sauce over them. Garnish with dill sprigs and lemon wedges. Serve with boiled new potatoes or buttered noodles.

Char-grilled Pork with Watercress

Succulent pork escalopes are coated in a honey, mustard and soy sauce glaze and then char-grilled. The addition of a smooth watercress sauce makes the dish complete.

Preparation time: 15 minutes
Cooking time: 20-25 minutes
Cals per serving: 500
Serves 4

1 medium onion	**30 ml (2 tbsp) dark soy sauce**
25g (1 oz) butter	**5 ml (1 tsp) paprika**
15 ml (1 tbsp) plain white flour	**grated rind and juice of 1 lemon**
150 ml (¼ pint) vegetable stock	**4 pork escalopes, each about 100g (4oz)**
150 ml (¼ pint) dry white wine	**2 bunches watercress**
½ red onion	**200ml (7 fl oz) crème fraîche or single cream**
60 ml (4 tbsp) thin honey	**salt and pepper**
30 ml (2 tbsp) Dijon mustard	

1 Fit the food processor with the metal blade. Peel and quarter the onion, place in the food processor and chop. Place in a saucepan with the butter and cook for 3-4 minutes until softened.

2 Stir in the flour, then gradually add the stock and wine. Bring to the boil stirring continuously. Cover and simmer for 5 minutes.

3 Meanwhile cut the red onion in half, add to the food processor and finely chop. Add the honey, mustard, soy sauce, paprika, lemon rind and juice and blend together. Transfer the glaze to a small bowl.

4 Brush both sides of the pork with the glaze and place on a grill rack. Grill under a medium heat for 10-12 minutes, turning over halfway through the cooking. Brush with glaze during the cooking.

5 Rinse the food processor bowl and metal blade. Reserve 4 sprigs of watercress and add the remainder to the processor with the wine sauce and blend until smooth. Return to the cleaned pan, stir in the crème fraîche or cream and reheat gently. Season to taste.

6 Serve the pork on warmed individual serving plates with the watercress sauce. Garnish with the reserved watercress sprigs.

Pork with Prunes and Mango

Pork is delicious cooked with fruit. This tender fillet of pork is stuffed with apples, dried mango, prunes and walnuts and served with a creamy Calvados sauce.

Preparation time: 20 minutes
Cooking time: 45-50 minutes
Cals per serving: 670-450
Serves 4-6

2 pork fillets, about 400 g (14 oz) each	**30 ml (2 tbsp) vegetable oil**
1 medium tart eating apple	**150 ml (¼ pint) single cream**
50 g (2 oz) dried mango slices or apricots	**45 ml (3 tbsp) Calvados**
175 g (6 oz) pitted ready to eat prunes	**150 ml (¼ pint) chicken stock**
50 g (2 oz) walnut halves	**salt and pepper**
5 ml (1 tsp) ground coriander	**TO GARNISH**
300 ml (½ pint) apple juice	**apple slices**
1 medium onion	**coriander sprigs**

1 Trim the pork fillets and split lengthways, without cutting right through. Open each out flat. Fit the grating disc. Peel, quarter and core the apple, then grate. Remove and set aside. Roughly chop the mango slices and 50 g (2 oz) prunes.

2 Fit the metal blade and roughly chop the walnuts. Add the chopped mango and prunes, grated apple, coriander and 30 ml (2 tbsp) apple juice. Briefly process to mix together. Spread the fruit stuffing over one pork fillet. Place the remaining fillet on top and tie at 2.5 cm (1 inch) intervals with string.

3 Preheat the oven to 200°C (400°F) Mark 6. Peel and quarter the onion. Using the metal blade roughly chop. Heat the oil in an ovenproof sauté pan or small roasting tin and sauté the onion, until softened. Set aside.

4 Add the pork to the pan and brown all over. Return the onion to the pan, add the remaining apple juice and prunes. Cover with foil and bake for 30 minutes. Uncover and cook for 10-15 minutes, or until tender.

5 Transfer the pork to a warmed dish and keep warm. Using the metal blade, purée the apple juice and prune mixture. Stir in the cream, Calvados and sufficient stock to give a thick pouring sauce. Season with salt and pepper to taste.

6 Serve the pork sliced with a little sauce. Garnish with apple slices and coriander. Serve the remaining sauce separately.

Piquant Chicken Pasta

Whole chicken breasts are baked in foil with butter, garlic, ginger and chilli to provide succulent slices of meat which are tossed with pasta, courgettes and fresh herbs.

Preparation time: 15 minutes
Cooking time: 35 minutes
Cals per serving: 640
Serves 4

4 cm (1½ inch) piece fresh root ginger	**coarse sea salt and pepper**
3 garlic cloves	**small bunch fresh coriander or tarragon**
1 red chilli	**4 sprigs fresh parsley**
4 boneless chicken breasts, skinned	**2 small courgettes**
65 g (2½ oz) butter	**400 g (14 oz) dried tagliatelle**

1 Preheat the oven to 190°C (375°F) Mark 5. Peel the ginger and cut in half. Peel the garlic cloves. Halve and deseed the chilli. Fit the metal blade. Put the ginger, garlic and chilli in the food processor and process for 20-30 seconds, or until finely chopped.

2 Arrange the chicken breasts in one layer on a large piece of foil and sprinkle with the chopped ginger, garlic and chilli. Dot with 25 g (1 oz) of the butter and season with salt and pepper.

3 Wrap the foil tightly to form a parcel and place on a baking sheet. Bake in the oven for 30 minutes, or until the chicken is tender and cooked through.

4 Meanwhile chop the coriander or tarragon and parsley using the metal blade. Remove and reserve. Fit the slicing disc and slice the courgettes.

5 Melt the remaining butter in a large frying pan. Add the courgettes and cook over a medium heat for 3-4 minutes until tender and just beginning to brown. Stir in the herbs and cook briefly. Remove from the heat.

6 About 5 minutes before the chicken is ready, cook the pasta in a large pan of boiling salted water until 'al dente' or according to the packet instructions.

7 When the chicken is cooked, carefully lift out, retaining the juices in the foil parcel. Cut the chicken into slices or cubes and return to the foil.

8 Drain the pasta and return to the pan. Add the chicken with its juices and the courgettes, butter and herbs. Toss lightly to mix. Adjust the seasoning to taste and serve at once.

Chicken with Cashews

A mild but spicy chicken dish, flavoured with mint, coriander, cumin and cardamom.
The ground cashew nuts add texture to the sauce.

Preparation time: 15 minutes
Cooking time: 50 minutes
Cals per serving: 400-270
Serves 4-6

about 1.4 kg (3 lb) chicken pieces, such as thighs and drumsticks	**4 cardamom pods**
2 large onions	**50 g (2 oz) cashew nuts**
2.5 cm (1 inch) piece fresh root ginger	**150 ml (¼ pint) thick yogurt**
1 garlic clove	**salt and pepper**
45 ml (3 tbsp) vegetable oil	**small bunch fresh coriander**
1 cinnamon stick	**6 sprigs fresh mint**
15 ml (1 tbsp) coriander seeds	**to serve**
10 ml (2 tsp) cumin seeds	**natural yogurt**
	garam masala

1 Skin the chicken pieces. If there are any large ones, such as breasts, cut into 2 or 3 pieces.

2 Peel and quarter the onions. Peel the ginger and garlic. Add all the vegetables to the food processor and finely chop, using the metal blade.

3 Heat the oil in a large flameproof casserole and add the chopped vegetables, cinnamon, coriander seeds, cumin seeds and cardamom pods. Cook over a high heat for 2-3 minutes, stirring all the time.

4 Put the cashew nuts in the food processor with 150 ml (¼ pint) cold water and process until smooth. Add to the pan and cook for 1-2 minutes. Add the chicken and stir to coat in spices.

5 Lower the heat then add the yogurt a spoonful at a time, followed by another 150 ml (¼ pint) water. Season with salt and pepper. Cover and cook gently for about 45 minutes, or until the chicken is cooked.

6 Place the coriander and mint in the food processor and chop finely. Add 75 ml (5 tbsp) to the saucepan and stir to combine. Check the seasoning. Serve each portion topped with a spoonful of yogurt and sprinkled with garam masala. Scatter with any remaining chopped herbs.

Chicken Vindaloo

This fiery curry originates from Southern India. Be sure to serve with a cooling yogurt and cucumber raita, as well as fluffy rice and naan bread or chapatis.

Preparation time: 20 minutes
Cooking time: About 1 hour
Cals per serving: 330
Serves 4

900 g (2 lb) chicken pieces such as thighs, drumsticks and breast fillets	**10 ml (2 tsp) black peppercorns**
2 medium onions	**5 ml (1 tsp) turmeric**
60 ml (4 tbsp) ghee or vegetable oil	**10 ml (2 tsp) sugar**
6 garlic cloves	**2.5 ml (½ tsp) salt**
2.5 cm (1 inch) piece fresh root ginger	**60 ml (4 tbsp) red wine vinegar**
10 ml (2 tsp) cumin seeds	**8 green cardamoms**
10 ml (2 tsp) coriander seeds	**1 cinnamon stick**
10 ml (2 tsp) fenugreek seeds	**4-6 dried red chillies**
	30 ml (2 tbsp) tomato purée

1 Remove the skin from the chicken and cut any large portions in half. Fit the metal blade. Peel and quarter the onions. Place in the food processor and roughly chop.

2 Heat 30 ml (2 tbsp) of the ghee in a frying pan. Add the onions and cook over a fairly high heat until golden brown, stirring all the time. Remove from the pan with a slotted spoon and drain on absorbent kitchen paper.

3 Peel the garlic cloves and ginger. Place in the food processor with the onions, cumin, coriander, fenugreek, peppercorns, turmeric, sugar, salt and vinegar. Process until smooth, then mix with the cardamoms, cinnamon and chillies.

4 Heat the remaining 30 ml (2 tbsp) ghee or vegetable oil in a large saucepan or casserole. Cook the chicken, in batches, on all sides. Add the vindaloo paste and stir so that the chicken is coated on all sides. Cook over a fairly high heat for about 5 minutes, stirring occasionally.

5 Add the tomato purée and 300 ml (½ pint) water. Bring to the boil, then lower the heat, cover and simmer for 45 minutes, or until the chicken is very tender.

6 Check from time to time to make sure that the sauce has not evaporated completely - if it looks too dry, simply add a little more water. If the chicken is cooked and the sauce is too thin, just cook it over a high heat for a few minutes to boil off some of the liquid. Check the seasoning and serve with rice.

Fruity Chicken Salad

Chicken poached with ginger and white wine is tossed in a creamy lime mayonnaise to make this delightful salad.

Preparation time: 30 minutes

Cooking time: 1¾ hours

Cals per serving: 515

Serves 6

1 chicken, about 1.6 kg (3½ lb)	**150 ml (¼ pint) double cream**
7.5 cm (3 inch) piece of fresh root ginger	**salt and pepper**
1 bouquet garni	**2 firm ripe pears**
300 ml (½ pint) dry white wine	**2 firm ripe kiwi fruits**
3 limes	**TO SERVE**
1 little gem lettuce	**mixed salad leaves and herbs**
4 spring onions	**lime slices, to garnish**
200 ml (7 fl oz) mayonnaise	

1 Put the chicken into a saucepan in which it fits snugly. Cut a small piece off the ginger and reserve. Crush the remainder with a rolling pin. Add to the pan with the bouquet garni, wine and the pared rind and juice of 1 lime. Pour over enough water to just cover the chicken.

2 Cover and bring to the boil. Simmer for 1½ hours or until tender. Skim off any scum and leave to cool. Remove the chicken from the pan and strain the liquid into a wide saucepan. Boil rapidly until reduced to about 150 ml (¼ pint).

3 Trim the lettuce and cut in half lengthways. Fit the slicing disc and finely shred the lettuce. Trim and slice the spring onions. Add both to the reduced liquid and cook for 1 minute, or until the lettuce has just wilted. Fit the metal blade and process until smooth. Leave to cool.

4 Meanwhile remove the chicken from the carcass, discarding all the skin and bone. Cut the meat into large bite-sized pieces.

5 Peel and grate the reserved ginger. Finely grate the rind from 1 lime. Mix into the puréed mixture with the ginger. Fold in the mayonnaise and cream. Add the juice of 1 lime, or to taste and season with salt and pepper.

6 Pour the dressing over the chicken and toss gently. Halve and core the pears. Cut into thick slices and toss in the juice of the remaining lime. Peel the kiwi fruits. Fit the medium or thick slicing disc and slice the kiwi.

7 Arrange the chicken, pears and kiwi on a bed of mixed salad leaves and herbs. Garnish with lime and serve with crusty bread.

Pheasant with Pecan Nuts

Pecan nuts and apple slices, sautéed in butter and sugar make a delicious garnish for this tender poached pheasant casserole. Serve with a seasonal green vegetable and jacket potatoes.

Preparation time: 25 minutes, plus marinating

Cooking time: 45-50 minutes

Cals per serving: 535

Serves 6

6 pheasant breasts, about 125 g (4 oz) each	**350 ml (12 fl oz) dry cider**
30 ml (2 tbsp) olive or walnut oil	**300 ml (½ pint) chicken stock**
1 medium carrot	**20 ml (4 tsp) light muscovado sugar**
1 medium leek	**salt and pepper**
1 medium onion	**3 Cox's apples**
75 g (3 oz) unsalted butter	**50 g (2 oz) pecan nuts**
15 ml (1 tbsp) plain white flour	

1 Place the pheasant breasts in a bowl, pour over the oil and stir well. Cover and leave to marinate in the refrigerator overnight.

2 Peel the carrot, trim the leek and peel and quarter the onion. Fit the slicing disc and slice the vegetables. Melt 50 g (2 oz) butter in a large flameproof casserole. Brown the pheasant breasts, three at a time and then set aside.

3 Sauté the sliced vegetables in the fat remaining in the casserole, for 4-5 minutes. Stir in the flour, cider, stock and half the sugar. Season with salt and pepper and bring to the boil, stirring.

4 Return all the pheasant breasts to the casserole, cover and simmer very gently for 30-35 minutes, or until very tender. Remove the pheasant with a slotted spoon.

5 Fit the metal blade. Put the vegetables and liquid in a food processor and blend until smooth. Return to the casserole with the pheasant. Cover and simmer gently for 5 minutes.

6 Meanwhile halve, core and thickly slice the apples. Sauté in the remaining butter with the pecan nuts and remaining sugar, for 2-3 minutes. Spoon over the pheasant and serve.

Turkey Pie

Herb flavoured scones make a tasty cobbler topping for this creamy turkey and ham pie.

Preparation time: 40 minutes
Cooking time: 40 minutes
Cals per serving: 735-550
Serves 6-8

700 g (1½ lb) cooked boneless turkey	**300 ml (½ pint) single cream**
225 g (8oz) piece cooked ham	**salt and pepper**
2 medium carrots	**HERB COBBLERS**
1 large leek	**8 sprigs fresh parsley**
900 ml (1½ pints) chicken stock	**small bunch fresh chives**
150 ml (¼ pint) dry white wine	**350 g (12 oz) self raising white flour**
2 fresh rosemary sprigs	**75 g (3 oz) butter**
125 g (4 oz) baby corn cobs	**about 200 ml (7 fl oz) milk**
225 g (8oz) chestnut or button mushrooms	**TO GARNISH**
75 g (3 oz) butter	**coarse sea salt**
60 ml (4 tbsp) plain white flour	**15 ml (1 tbsp) rosemary leaves**

1 Cut the turkey and ham into bite-sized pieces. Place in a 1.7 litre (3 pint) ovenproof dish. Peel the carrots. Fit the thick slicing disc and slice the carrots and leek.

2 Put the stock, wine and rosemary into a saucepan and bring to the boil. Add the carrots and cook for 10 minutes. Add the leeks and baby corn cobs and cook for 5-8 minutes, or until tender. Strain the stock into a jug and add the vegetables to the meat.

3 Quarter the mushrooms. Melt the butter in a saucepan, add the mushrooms and cook for 3-4 minutes. Stir in the flour, off the heat then stir in the stock and cream. Bring to the boil, stirring. Simmer for 5 minutes and season. Mix with the meat. Cool.

4 Preheat oven to 220°C (425°F) Mark 7. Using the metal blade chop the parsley and chives. Set aside. Place the flour, 2.5 ml (½ tsp) salt and butter in the food processor and process until it resembles fine breadcrumbs. Add the herbs and sufficient milk to make a soft scone mixture. Process briefly until just combined.

5 On a floured surface roll out to 1 cm (½ inch) thickness and cut out nine 7.5 cm (3 inch) squares. Halve diagonally. Arrange overlapping, around the edge of the dish brush with milk and sprinkle with sea salt.

6 Bake for 10 minutes then lower the temperature to 190°C (375°F) Mark 5. Bake for 15 minutes, sprinkle with rosemary leaves and bake for a further 15 minutes.

Duck Breasts with Rösti

Rösti potato cakes flavoured with apple are topped with tender pink slices of duck and then drizzled with a little apple flavoured sauce.

Preparation time: 30 minutes

Cooking time: 20-25 minutes

Cals per serving: 430

Serves 4

2 large duck breast fillets, each about 350 g (12 oz), or 4 medium duck breast fillets	**1 dessert apple**
salt and pepper	**2 fresh sage leaves**
15 ml (1 tbsp) red wine vinegar	**oil, for frying**
60 ml (4 tbsp) apple juice	**TO GARNISH**
RÖSTI	**sautéed apple slices**
450 g (1 lb) old potatoes	**sage sprigs**

1 Use a sharp knife to score through the skin side of the duck. Rub with salt and pepper. Leave at room temperature for 15 minutes.

2 To make the rösti, peel the potatoes and apple. Fit the grating disc and grate the potatoes and apple. Squeeze out as much moisture as possible and place in a bowl. Chop the sage and mix with the potato and apple. Season well with salt and pepper.

3 Preheat the oven to 150°C (300°F) Mark 2. Heat 15 ml (1 tbsp) oil in a small heavy-based frying pan. Place 2 large tablespoonfuls of the potato mixture in the pan, pressing down hard with a fish slice. Cook for 2 minutes or until golden brown on the underside; turn over and cook until crisp and golden. Remove and drain on absorbent kitchen paper. Repeat with the remaining mixture until you have at least 8 rösti. Keep warm in the oven while cooking the duck.

4 Preheat a heavy flameproof casserole. Add the duck breasts skin-side down and cook over a medium heat for 7-10 minutes depending on size, without moving them; the fat which runs out will prevent them sticking. Turn the breasts over and cook for 3-4 minutes, depending on size.

5 Using a slotted spoon, transfer the duck breasts to a warmed serving dish, Cover and leave in the warm oven for 10 minutes to relax and become evenly 'rosy' inside. Meanwhile pour off all the fat from the pan. Add the wine vinegar and apple juice. Bring to the boil and reduce slightly.

6 To serve, place two rösti on each warmed serving plate. Slice the duck thickly and arrange evenly on top of the rösti. Spoon on the sauce and serve immediately, garnished with sautéed apple slices and sage.

VEGETARIAN DISHES

Golden Onion Tart

Thinly sliced onions are fried until golden to make the filling for this tart. A creamy Cheddar and Parmesan cheese custard is poured over the onions and the tart is baked until golden.

Preparation time: 30 minutes, plus cooling
Cooking time: 1-1¼ hours
Cals per serving: 530
Serves 6

PASTRY	25 g (1 oz) Parmesan cheese
100 g (4 oz) butter	125 g (4 oz) mature Cheddar cheese
175 g (6 oz) plain white flour	2 eggs and 1 egg yolk
pinch salt	150 ml (¼ pint) single cream
FILLING	150 ml (¼ pint) milk
700 g (1½ lb) onions	pinch grated nutmeg
50 g (2 oz) butter	salt and pepper

1 Fit the metal blade. Dice the butter and place in the food processor with the flour and salt. Process for a few seconds until the mixture resembles fine breadcrumbs.

2 Add 30-45 ml (2-3 tbsp) cold water and process for 20-30 seconds or until the pastry clings together and forms a ball. Transfer to a lightly floured surface and knead gently to form a smooth ball. Wrap and chill for 20 minutes. Preheat the oven to 200°C (400°F) Mark 6.

3 On a lightly floured surface, roll out the pastry and use to line a 23 cm (9 inch), loose-based fluted flan tin. Place on a baking sheet. Prick the base. Line with greaseproof paper and baking beans and bake blind for 15-20 minutes, until lightly browned, removing the paper and beans for the last 5 minutes.

4 Meanwhile make the filling. Fit the slicing disc. Peel the onions and slice. Melt the butter in a frying pan, add the onions and stir thoroughly. Cover and cook over a moderate heat for 20-25 minutes, until soft and golden. Stir once or twice.

5 Fit the grating disc and grate the cheeses. Remove and set aside. Fit the metal blade, add the eggs, egg yolk, cream, milk, nutmeg and seasoning and process until well mixed. Reserve 75 ml (3 tbsp) grated cheese. Add the remainder and use the pulse switch to just mix them in.

6 Reduce the oven to 180°C (350°F) Mark 4. Spoon the onions into the flan case. Pour the egg mixture over and sprinkle with the reserved grated cheese. Bake for 35-40 minutes, or until just set. Cool for 15 minutes before serving warm.

Filo Mushroom Tartlets

Crispy layers of wafer-thin pastry encase a tasty mushroom filling, topped with a lightly baked egg. Serve as a snack or with mixed salad for a main course.

Preparation time: 30 minutes
Cooking time: 25-30 minutes
Cals per serving: 375
Serves 6

8-10 sheets filo pastry	**125 g (4 oz) flat mushrooms**
15 ml (1 tbsp) sunflower oil	**5 sun-dried tomatoes in oil**
FILLING	**4 sprigs fresh parsley**
2 small red onions	**10 ml (2 tsp) lemon juice**
2 garlic cloves	**salt and pepper**
15 ml (1 tbsp) sunflower oil	**6 eggs**
125 g (4 oz) chestnut mushrooms	

1 Preheat the oven to 190°C (375°F) Mark 5. Lightly grease six 9 cm (3½ inch), 2.5 cm (1 inch) deep flan tins. Cut the filo pastry into 18 squares, each 11 cm (4½ inches). Brush each square with a little sunflower oil.

2 Layer 3 sheets in each tin, arranging them at an angle to each other so the points form a star. Press the pastry into the sides of the tin. Bake for 10-15 minutes, until golden and crispy. (Don't overcook them as they have to be baked again).

3 To make the filling, peel the onions and garlic. Fit the metal blade and finely chop the onions. Heat the oil, add the onions and fry until softened and transparent. Using the metal blade finely chop the garlic and mushrooms and add to the pan. Cook until the juices start to run.

4 Drain the tomatoes and place in the food processor with the parsley and chop finely. Stir into the cooked mushrooms with the lemon juice. Season to taste. Divide between the prepared pastry cases.

5 Make a well in the centre of the filling with the back of a spoon, pushing the filling to the side. Break one egg into a small saucer or cup, then slide into the well. Repeat with the remainder.

6 Return to the oven and cook for 14-16 minutes, until the eggs are softly set and creamy, depending on how you prefer them cooked. Serve immediately.

Caerphilly Cheese Sausages

Caerphilly cheese, breadcrumbs, spring onions and herbs are mixed together to make these vegetarian sausages. They taste delicious served with the watercress and apple salad.

Preparation time: 15 minutes

Cooking time: 10 minutes

Cals per serving: 705

Serves 4

125 g (4 oz) Caerphilly cheese	10 ml (2 tsp) mustard powder
6 sprigs fresh parsley	oil for shallow frying
2 spring onions	**WATERCRESS AND APPLE SALAD**
200 g (7 oz) crustless white bread	1 small red onion
2.5 ml (½ tsp) dried thyme	2 green eating apples
salt and pepper	50 g (2 oz) watercress
freshly grated nutmeg	75 g (3 oz) walnut halves
2 eggs	15 ml (1 tbsp) sherry vinegar
a little milk, if necessary	45 ml (3 tbsp) olive oil
45 ml (3 tbsp) plain white flour	15 ml (1 tbsp) walnut oil

1 Fit the grating disc and grate the cheese. Set aside. Fit the metal blade and chop the parsley and onions. Tear the bread into pieces, and process into breadcrumbs. Add the cheese, thyme, salt, pepper and nutmeg. Process for a few seconds on pulse to mix.

2 Separate one egg, placing the egg white in a shallow dish. In another bowl mix the egg yolk with the remaining whole egg, add to the processor and mix together. If necessary, moisten with a little milk, the mixture must be soft enough to gather into balls.

3 Divide into 8 and shape each one into a cylindrical sausage. Beat the reserved egg white until lightly frothy. Mix the flour and mustard together on a plate.

4 Brush the sausages with the egg white, then, using 2 forks, roll them in the flour and mustard. Heat the oil in a frying pan and fry the sausages slowly until cooked right through, turning frequently. Drain on kitchen paper.

5 Meanwhile peel and halve the onion. Quarter and core the apple. Fit the slicing disc and slice the onion and apple. Toss together with the watercress and half the walnuts. Fit the metal blade and finely chop the remaining walnuts. Add the vinegar, olive and walnut oils and seasoning and process for a few seconds, to combine.

6 Arrange the salad on serving plates and drizzle with walnut vinaigrette. Serve the sausages, piping hot, with the salad.

Falafel with Sesame Dressing

These Eastern chick pea fritters make a delicious light meal served with a leafy salad.

Preparation time: 25 minutes, plus soaking
Cooking time: about 30 minutes
Cals per serving: 430-290
Serves 4-6

150 g (5 oz) dried chick peas	**DRESSING**
1 bunch spring onions	**15 ml (1 tbsp) sesame seeds**
3 garlic cloves	**1 red chilli**
6 sprigs fresh parsley	**30 ml (2 tbsp) sesame oil**
8 sprigs fresh coriander	**30 ml (2 tbsp) sunflower oil**
5 ml (1 tsp) cumin seeds	**finely grated rind and juice 1 lime**
2.5 ml (½ tsp) baking powder	**10 ml (2 tsp) caster sugar**
salt and pepper	**TO GARNISH**
oil for shallow frying	**flat leaf parsley**
	lime wedges

1 Cover the chick peas with plenty of cold water. Leave to soak overnight. Drain, place in a saucepan with plenty of fresh water and boil rapidly for 15 minutes. Drain.

2 Meanwhile make the dressing. Heat the sesame seeds in a frying pan until golden. Halve the chilli, remove the seeds and roughly chop. Fit the metal blade. Blend together the chilli, oils, lime rind and juice and sugar until chilli is finely chopped. Season with salt. Stir in the sesame seeds and transfer to a small serving dish.

3 Trim and roughly chop the spring onions. Using the cleaned food processor fitted with the metal blade, blend the chick peas with the spring onions, garlic, herbs, cumin, baking powder and a little seasoning, until it forms a coarse paste.

4 Shape the chick pea mixture into little patties. Heat a 1 cm (½ inch) depth of oil in a large frying pan. Using 2 spoons, lower the patties into the pan. Fry, several at a time, until golden on the underside. Turn over and cook until golden.

5 Drain on absorbent kitchen paper and keep warm while cooking the remainder. Garnish with parsley and lime and serve with the dressing.

NOTE: The falafel mixture needs to be made with freshly cooked dried chick-peas. Tinned chick peas make the falafel mixture too soft and tend to break up during frying.

Pasta with Pecan and Basil

There may not seem to be a lot of sauce in this recipe, but it is very rich, so a little goes a long way. Serve this pasta with a selection of roasted or stir-fried vegetables.

Preparation time: 15 minutes

Cooking time: 12 minutes

Cals per serving: 480

Serves 4

50 g (2 oz) Parmesan cheese	350 g (12 oz) fresh pasta or 225 g (8 oz) dried
2 large garlic cloves	50 g (2 oz) walnut pieces
1 medium tomato	45 ml (3 tbsp) single cream
large bunch fresh basil leaves, about 40 g (1½ oz)	**TO SERVE**
60 ml (4 tbsp) olive oil	fresh basil sprigs
salt and pepper	freshly grated Parmesan cheese

1 Fit the grating disc and grate the Parmesan cheese. Peel the garlic. Skin the tomato, cut in half and remove the seeds.

2 Fit the metal blade. Add the garlic, basil and tomato flesh and process to a smooth paste. With the food processor running, gradually add the olive oil, drop by drop, through the feed tube. Stop when all the oil has been added and the mixture is thick. Season with salt and pepper.

3 Cook the pasta in a large pan of boiling salted water until 'al dente' or according to the packet instructions. Drain well.

4 Roughly chop the walnuts. Add to the pasta, with the basil sauce and cream. Toss together and serve on warmed plates, garnished with basil sprigs and sprinkled with Parmesan cheese.

Fusilli with Cheesy Pumpkin

Pumpkin is mixed with dolcelatte cheese and cream to make this rich pasta dish. Serve with a simple tossed salad. Use a firm-fleshed squash, such as acorn or butternut squash, when pumpkin is out of season.

Preparation time: 15 minutes
Cooking time: About 20 minutes
Cals per serving: 930-620

Serves 4-6

350 g (12 oz) wedge pumpkin	**400 g (14 oz) dried fusilli, pappardelle or tagliatelle**
25 g (1 oz) butter	**175 g (6 oz) dolcelatte cheese**
1 garlic clove	**salt and pepper**
small bunch of fresh parsley	**TO GARNISH**
300 ml (½ pint) extra-thick double cream	**30 ml (2 tbsp) toasted pine nuts**
1.25 ml (¼ tsp) freshly grated nutmeg	

1 Fit the grating disc. Discard the seeds and remove the skin from the pumpkin. Using the food processor grate the flesh.

2 Melt the butter in a large frying pan. Add the grated pumpkin. Peel and crush the garlic and add to the frying pan. Cook over a medium heat, stirring, for about 5 minutes, until softened.

3 Fit the metal blade and finely chop the parsley. Stir the cream, nutmeg and 30 ml (2 tbsp) chopped parsley into the pumpkin mixture. Cook for 2 minutes. Keep the remaining chopped parsley for garnish.

4 Cook the pasta in a large pan of boiling salted water until 'al dente' or according to the packet instructions.

5 Cut the dolcelatte into small pieces and add to the sauce. Heat gently, stirring until melted. Season with salt and pepper to taste.

6 To serve, drain the pasta thoroughly in a colander and return to the pan. Add the sauce and toss well to mix. Transfer to a warmed serving bowl or plates and serve at once, sprinkled with toasted pine nuts and any remaining chopped parsley.

Spinach and Feta Cheese Pizza

This pizza is topped with spinach, mushrooms and tomatoes. Vary the vegetables depending on your likes and dislikes. Include some sliced courgettes or peppers for a change.

Preparation time: 30 minutes
Cooking time: 25 minutes
Cals per serving: 600

Serves 4

PIZZA DOUGH	125 g (4 oz) chestnut mushrooms
175 g (6 oz) strong plain white flour	2 garlic cloves
50 g (2 oz) plain wholemeal flour	450 g (1 lb) baby spinach leaves
50 g (2 oz) semolina	90 ml (6 tbsp) sun-dried tomato paste
pinch of salt	75 g (3 oz) feta cheese
15 g (½ oz) butter or margarine	175 g (6 oz) grated mozzarella cheese
15 ml (1 tbsp) finely chopped fresh rosemary	pepper
15 g (½ oz) fast action dried yeast	12 black olives
TOPPING	15 ml (1 tbsp) olive oil
3 medium tomatoes	

1 Fit the dough blade or hook. Place the flours, semolina, salt and butter in the food processor. Process for a few seconds to blend. Add the rosemary and yeast.

2 With the processor running, add 200 ml (7 fl oz) warm water in through the feed tube. Within 15-20 seconds a ball of dough will form; continue for a further 25 seconds. Turn out onto a lightly floured surface, knead lightly, roll out into 30 cm (12 inch) circle and place on a greased baking sheet. Cover with lightly oiled polythene and leave in a warm place to rise for 30 minutes.

3 Meanwhile prepare the topping. Fit the medium or thick slicing disc and slice the tomatoes and mushrooms. Peel and crush the garlic.

4 Wash the spinach thoroughly, drain and place in a saucepan. Cover and cook for 3 minutes, until wilted. Refresh under cold running water, and squeeze out the excess moisture.

5 Preheat the oven to 220°C (425°F) Mark 7. Spread the sun-dried tomato paste over the pizza base. Top with the spinach, mushrooms and tomatoes. Crumble the feta cheese and mix with the mozzarella cheese. Sprinkle over the vegetables with the garlic.

6 Grind over some black pepper, scatter with olives and drizzle over a little olive oil. Bake in the oven for 20 minutes, until well risen. Transfer to a serving plate and serve with a crisp green salad.

Tomato Crêpes with Antipasto

Sun-dried tomato paste adds a delicious bite to these savoury pancakes, finished with a spicy pepper and tomato filling. They are served with a garlic yogurt sauce.

Preparation time: 35 minutes

Cooking time: 30 minutes

Cals per serving: 755-537

Serves 4-6

125 g (4 oz) plain white flour	**5 ml (1 tsp) chilli powder**
45 ml (3 tbsp) sun-dried tomato paste	**2 x 190 g jars mixed pepper in tomato dressing antipasto**
1 egg	
salt and pepper	**SAUCE**
300 ml (½ pint) milk	**2 garlic cloves**
oil for frying	**150 ml (¼ pint) Greek-style yogurt**
FILLING	**TO GARNISH**
450 g (1 lb) plum tomatoes	**parsley sprigs**
175 g (6 oz) Pecorino cheese	**basil sprigs**
60 ml (4 tbsp) olive oil	

1 Fit the metal blade. Add the flour, tomato paste, egg, a little salt and pepper and half the milk to the food processor. Process for a few seconds, until smooth. Gradually add the remaining milk through the feed tube and process until smooth. Pour into a jug.

2 Fit the slicing disc and slice the tomatoes for the filling. Set aside. Fit the grating disc and grate the cheese. Mix the olive oil and chilli powder together.

3 Heat a medium frying pan with a little oil until very hot. Drain off the excess oil, pour a little of the batter into the pan and tilt to coat the base. Cook over a moderate heat until the underside is golden. Turn over and cook the other side. Repeat to make 8 pancakes.

4 Preheat the oven to 180°C (350°F) Mark 4. Arrange the sliced tomatoes over the pancakes and brush with the chilli oil. Spread the antipasto on top. Scatter with all but 60 ml (4 tbsp) of the cheese.

5 Fold each pancake into quarters to enclose the filling. Arrange in a large shallow baking dish and scatter with the remaining cheese. Bake for 20 minutes until hot.

6 Make the yogurt sauce. Peel and crush the garlic and mix with the yogurt. Season lightly and transfer to a small serving dish. Serve the pancakes garnished with parsley and basil sprigs. Serve with the garlic yogurt.

Vegetable and Lentil Casserole

This warming winter supper dish, combines a mixture of root vegetables with lentils and spices.
Serve with a green vegetable or a side salad.

Preparation time: 20 minutes
Cooking time: 45 minutes
Cals per serving: 260
Serves 6

25 g (1 oz) fresh root ginger	**350 g (12 oz) leeks**
2 garlic cloves	**450 g (1 lb) button mushrooms**
5 ml (1 tsp) cumin seeds	**45 ml (3 tbsp) olive oil**
15 ml (1 tbsp) coriander seeds	**1.25 ml (¼ tsp) turmeric**
5 ml (1 tsp) mustard seeds	**175 g (6 oz) split red lentils**
2 medium onions	**50 g (2 oz) brown or green lentils**
450 g (1 lb) carrots	**salt and pepper**
350 g (12 oz) mooli (white radish)	**small bunch fresh coriander**

1 Preheat the oven to 180°C (350°F) Mark 4. Fit the metal blade. Peel the ginger and garlic. Add the cumin seeds, coriander seeds, mustard seeds, ginger and garlic to the food processor and process until finely chopped. Remove and set aside.

2 Peel and halve the onions. Peel the carrots and mooli. Clean the leeks. Fit the thick slicing blade and slice the onions, carrots, mooli and leeks. Halve the mushrooms if large.

3 Heat the oil in a flameproof casserole. Add the onions, carrots, mooli and leeks and fry for 2-3 minutes, stirring constantly. Add the mushrooms, spice mix and turmeric and fry for 1 minute, stirring.

4 Rinse the lentils in a colander under cold running water, then drain. Stir the lentils into the casserole with 750 ml (1¼ pints) boiling water. Season with salt and pepper and return to the boil. Cover and cook in the oven for about 30 minutes or until the vegetables and lentils are tender.

5 Fit the metal blade and finely chop the coriander. Stir into the casserole, adjust the seasoning and serve.

Lentil and Potato Pie

Puy lentils, tossed with a mixture of vegetables, garlic, plenty of herbs and a creamy stock,
makes a wonderful filling for this potato pastry topped pie.

Preparation time: 30 minutes plus cooling
Cooking time: 1½ hours
Cals per serving: 675
Serves 6

175 g (6 oz) Puy lentils	150 ml (¼ pint) double cream
450 ml (¾ pint) vegetable stock	salt and pepper
2 medium leeks	PASTRY
3 sticks celery	300 g (10 oz) potatoes
1 medium onion	150 g (5 oz) butter
3 medium carrots	300 g (10 oz) plain white flour
6 garlic cloves	2.5 ml (½ tsp) salt
60 ml (4 tbsp) olive oil	beaten egg, to glaze
6 sprigs fresh parsley	coarse sea salt, to sprinkle
6 sprigs fresh oregano	

1 Place the lentils in a saucepan, cover with cold water and bring to the boil. Boil rapidly for 10 minutes. Drain and place in the cleaned pan with the stock. Bring to the boil, cover and simmer gently for 10 minutes.

2 Trim the leeks and celery. Peel and halve the onion. Peel the carrots and garlic. Fit the slicing blade and slice the leeks, celery, onion, carrots and garlic.

3 Heat the olive oil in a large pan, add the vegetables and fry for 8 minutes, stirring. Fit the metal blade and roughly chop the parsley and oregano. Add the lentils, stock, herbs, cream and salt and pepper to season. Turn into a large, shallow pie dish and leave to cool.

4 Make the pastry. Peel the potatoes and cut into chunks. Cook in boiling water for 10 minutes, or until tender. Drain and mash. Dice the butter and using the metal blade blend together the butter, flour and salt until the mixture resembles fine breadcrumbs.

5 Add the potato and 20 ml (4 tsp) cold water. Process until mixture forms a dough, adding more water if necessary. Preheat the oven to 200°C (400°F) Mark 6.

6 Roll out pastry on a lightly floured surface and use to cover the pie. Trim off the excess pastry and use to decorate the pie. Make a hole in the centre for the steam to escape. Brush with beaten egg, scatter with sea salt and bake for 40 minutes, until the pastry is golden.

Okra and Aubergine Pilaf

A tangy mango sauce provides a refreshing contrast to the rich flavours of this delicious pilaf.

Preparation time: 25 minutes, plus standing time

Cooking time: 30 minutes

Cals per serving: 610

Serves 4

175 g (6 oz) okra	300 ml (½ pint) vegetable stock
1 medium aubergine	**RELISH**
salt and pepper	10 ml (2 tsp) black mustard seeds
2 red onions	1 shallot
2 garlic cloves	small bunch fresh coriander
4 cm (1½ inch) piece fresh root ginger	small bunch fresh parsley
25 g (1 oz) pine nuts	1 medium mango
90 ml (6 tbsp) olive oil	30 ml (2 tbsp) white wine vinegar
225 g (8 oz) long grain rice	5 ml (1 tsp) light soft brown sugar

1 Slice the okra, diagonally into 2.5 cm (1 inch) lengths. Cut the aubergine into small chunks. Place in a colander with plenty of salt and leave for 30 minutes. Rinse in cold water and dry thoroughly. Peel and quarter the onions. Peel the garlic and ginger. Fit the metal blade and finely chop the onions, garlic and ginger. Remove and set aside.

2 Meanwhile make the relish. Lightly crush the mustard seeds and heat in a frying pan until they pop. Peel the shallot and quarter. Using the metal blade roughly chop the coriander and parsley. Add the mustard seeds and shallot and lightly blend. Halve, peel and stone the mango. Roughly chop the flesh. Add to the food processor with the vinegar and sugar. Blend until finely chopped. Turn into a small serving dish.

3 Cook the pine nuts in a large frying pan, until golden. Remove and set aside. Add 15 ml (1 tbsp) oil to the pan and fry the okra for 4-5 minutes, until beginning to brown. Remove and set aside.

4 Add 60 ml (4 tbsp) oil and fry the onion mixture and aubergines for 8-10 minutes, until browned. Remove and set aside. Add the remaining oil to the pan. Add the rice and cook for 1 minute, stirring. Add the stock, bring to the boil, cover and cook for 5 minutes.

5 Add the aubergine, okra, onions and pine nuts and cook for a further 5 minutes, or until the rice is tender. Season to taste and serve with the relish.

VEGETABLE ACCOMPANIMENTS AND SALADS

Red Cabbage with Cranberries

Slowly cooked red cabbage flavoured with spices and cranberries. A perfect accompaniment to pork, game or turkey.

Preparation time: 10 minutes
Cooking time: 1¾ hours
Cals per serving: 125
Serves 6

1 large onion	**40 g (1½ oz) soft dark brown sugar**
50 g (2 oz) butter	**5 ml (1 tsp) mixed spice**
700 g (1½ lb) red cabbage	**125 g (4 oz) fresh or frozen cranberries**
30 ml (2 tbsp) white wine vinegar	**salt and pepper**

1 Preheat the oven to 170°C (325°F) Mark 3. Peel the onion and quarter. Fit the slicing disc and slice the onion. Melt the butter in an ovenproof casserole and sauté the onion for 10 minutes, until softened.

2 Cut the cabbage into quarters and discard the core. Cut the quarters in half again and slice using the slicing disc. Add to the casserole with the vinegar, sugar, mixed spice, cranberries and seasoning. Mix together and cook for 1½ hours, or until cabbage is tender.

Brussels Sprouts with Bacon

These shredded Brussels sprouts are stir-fried with bacon. Serve with roasts or cold meats.

Preparation time: 10 minutes
Cooking time: 7 minutes
Cals per serving: 300
Serves 4

700 g (1½ lb) Brussels sprouts	**10 ml (2 tsp) caraway seeds**
175 g (6 oz) piece smoked bacon	**salt and pepper**
50 g (2 oz) butter	**freshly grated nutmeg**
60 ml (4 tbsp) double cream	

1 Fit the slicing disc. Trim the Brussels sprouts, then use the food processor to shred them very finely.

2 Fit the metal blade. Remove the rind from the bacon and cut into large chunks. Place in the food processor and roughly chop.

3 Heat a wok or frying pan and add the bacon. Cook over a high heat, stirring all the time, until the fat runs and the bacon is brown and crisp. Stir in the butter.

4 Toss in the Brussels sprouts and stir-fry over a high heat for 2-3 minutes, until they begin to wilt. Stir in the cream, add the caraway seeds and stir-fry for 1 minute. Season with salt, pepper and nutmeg. Transfer to a warmed serving dish and serve immediately.

Puréed Root Vegetables

A tasty winter vegetable dish, this recipe uses a combination of root vegetables, which are cooked and then puréed together. Try different root vegetables, such as celeriac, turnip or sweet potato.

Preparation time: 15 minutes
Cooking time: 25 minutes
Cals per serving: 185
Serves 6

450 g (1 lb) potatoes	**25 g (1 oz) butter**
450 g (1 lb) parsnips	**salt and pepper**
450 g (1 lb) carrots	**TO GARNISH**
1.1 litres (2 pints) vegetable stock	**snipped chives**
300 ml (½ pint) very low fat fromage frais	

1 Peel and roughly chop the potatoes, parsnips and carrots into even sized pieces. Bring the stock to the boil in a large saucepan, add the vegetables, cover and cook for about 20 minutes, or until tender.

2 Fit the metal blade. Drain the vegetables and place in the food processor with the fromage frais. Process to a smooth purée. Return to the cleaned saucepan with the butter. Stir over a moderate heat until piping hot. Season and serve garnished with snipped chives.

Potato and Parsnip Galette

Golden slices of potato and parsnip flavoured with a hint of honey and lemon make this buttery vegetable cake. It is a perfect partner to roasts and game dishes.

Preparation time: 25 minutes
Cooking time: 45 minutes
Cals per serving: 380
Serves 6

900 g (2 lb) firm potatoes, such as Desirée, Romano, Estima or Wilja	**60 ml (4 tbsp) thin honey**
225 g (8 oz) young parsnips	**30 ml (2 tbsp) lemon juice**
175 g (6 oz) butter	**freshly grated nutmeg**
	salt and pepper

1. Preheat the oven to 200°C (400°F) Mark 6. Peel the potatoes and parsnips. Fit the slicing disc and thinly slice the potatoes and parsnips. Do not rinse the potatoes to remove the starch as it is needed to help the potatoes stick together. Divide the potatoes into three. Don't worry if they discolour.

2. To clarify the butter, slowly melt in a small saucepan, then skim off any white residue or foam; keep warm. Melt the honey and lemon juice together in a small pan and keep warm.

3. Pour 30 ml (2 tbsp) butter into a heavy 20 cm (8 inch) non-stick frying pan, with an integral metal handle, which is suitable for oven use. Layer one third of the potatoes over the bottom of the pan, in neat overlapping circles, seasoning well.

4. Lay half the sliced parsnips over the potato layer. Brush with honey and lemon juice and season with nutmeg, salt and pepper.

5. Cover with another third of the potato slices, brushing with butter and seasoning well. Layer the remaining parsnips on top. Brush with the remaining honey and lemon juice, and season with nutmeg, salt and pepper. Finish with the remaining potato slices, brushing with butter and seasoning. Pour over any remaining butter.

6. Place the pan over a medium heat and cook carefully for about 5 minutes, or until the underside begins to turn golden brown. Test by carefully lifting up the edge with a palette knife.

7. Press the potatoes down firmly and cover with a lid or buttered kitchen foil. Bake for 40-45 minutes or until the potatoes and parsnips are tender when pierced with a sharp knife and the underside is deep golden brown.

8. Loosen the galette with a palette knife. Place a warmed serving plate over the pan and quickly invert the galette onto the dish. Serve immediately.

Spring Vegetable Stir-fry

A colourful mix of spring vegetables stir-fried together and then tossed in a mustard and basil laced French dressing.

Preparation time: 20 minutes
Cooking time: 20 minutes
Cals per serving: 155
Serves 6

225 g (8 oz) small new potatoes	**DRESSING**
225 g (8 oz) carrots	**45 ml (3 tbsp) olive oil**
125 g (4 oz) French beans	**15 ml (1 tbsp) white wine vinegar**
225 g (8 oz) broccoli	**5 ml (1 tsp) Dijon mustard**
1 garlic clove	**salt and pepper**
1 medium red pepper	**TO GARNISH**
175 g (6 oz) courgettes	**shredded basil leaves**
30 ml (2 tbsp) olive oil	

1 Scrub the potatoes and cook in a saucepan of boiling salted water for 10 minutes, or until just tender. Drain and set aside.

2 Peel the carrots and cut into 5 cm (2 inch) pieces. Fit the stir-fry or chipper disc and cut the carrots into thin strips. If the chipper disc is large, use a very coarse 8 mm grating disc instead. Cut the French beans in half. Trim the broccoli and cut into florets. Peel and crush the garlic.

3 Quarter, core and deseed the pepper. Using the stir-fry disc, cut into thin strips. Remove and set aside. Cut the courgettes into 5 cm (2 inch) pieces and then cut into thin strips using the stir-fry disc.

4 Heat the olive oil in a large frying pan or wok. Add the garlic, carrots and beans and stir-fry for 2 minutes. Add the broccoli and pepper and stir-fry for another 2 minutes. Add the courgettes and potatoes and cook for a further 2 minutes.

5 Meanwhile combine the dressing ingredients in a screw top jar and shake. Transfer the vegetables to a warm serving dish and pour over the dressing. Garnish with shredded basil leaves and serve.

Potato and Camembert Gratin

A rich and creamy potato gratin. The food processor makes light work of slicing the potatoes and onions.

Preparation time: 10 minutes
Cooking time: 1¾-2 hours
Cals per serving: 425
Serves 6

melted butter, for greasing	**200 ml (7 fl oz) crème fraîche**
1 large onion	**300 ml (½ pint) single cream**
25 g (1 oz) butter	**salt and pepper**
700 g (1½ lb) old potatoes	**150 g (5 oz) Camembert cheese**

1 Grease a 1.4 litre (2½ pint) gratin dish with the melted butter.

2 Peel the onion and cut into quarters. Fit the slicing disc and slice the onion. Melt the butter in a frying pan, add the onion slices and sauté for 10 minutes, until softened.

3 Preheat the oven to 150°C (300°F) Mark 2. Scrub the potatoes, cut in half, if necessary, to fit the food processor feed tube and slice.

4 Mix the crème fraîche, cream and salt and pepper together in a saucepan and heat gently until hot. Remove the rind from the cheese and cut into thin slices.

5 Arrange a layer of overlapping potatoes in the prepared dish. Arrange half the onions and cheese on top. Repeat the layers, finishing with a layer of potatoes. Pour over the cream mixture.

6 Place the dish on a baking sheet and bake for 1½- 1¾ hours, until golden brown and tender.

Asparagus with Lime Hollandaise

A speedy method for making hollandaise sauce. Serve this delightful asparagus with poached or baked fish.

Preparation time: 20 minutes
Cooking time: 15-20 minutes
Cals per serving: 265

Serves 6

900 g (2 lb) asparagus	175 g (6 oz) unsalted butter
salt and pepper	3 egg yolks
dash of lemon juice	small bunch fresh chervil
HOLLANDAISE SAUCE	grated rind and juice of 1 lime
45 ml (3 tbsp) white wine vinegar	salt and pepper
6 black peppercorns	TO GARNISH
1 bay leaf	chervil sprigs

1 Trim the asparagus, discarding the woody ends. Tie into 4 equal bundles and stand, tips upwards in a large saucepan of boiling salted water. Add the lemon juice, cover and simmer for 7-10 minutes, or until tender.

2 Meanwhile make the hollandaise. Place the vinegar, peppercorns and bay leaf in a small saucepan. Bring to the boil and boil until reduced by half. Remove the peppercorns and bay leaf and set aside. Place the butter in a saucepan and melt.

3 Fit the metal blade and place the egg yolks and chervil in the bowl. With the machine running, and, through the feed tube, slowly add half the hot melted butter. Add the reduced vinegar, lime rind and juice and finally the remaining butter. Process for a further 20 seconds, or until the sauce is smooth and creamy. Season with salt and pepper.

4 Drain the asparagus. Place in a large, warmed serving dish and pour over the hollandaise sauce. Garnish with chervil and serve.

Spiced Coleslaw with Pecans

This coleslaw is made with a chilli and mango flavoured dressing, to give a spicy twist to an ever-popular recipe. The food processor makes light work of the grating and shredding.

Preparation time: 15 minutes, plus standing
Cooking time: Nil
Cals per serving: 340
Serves 4

350 g (12 oz) white cabbage	30 ml (2 tbsp) wine vinegar
2-3 celery sticks	10 ml (2 tsp) mango chutney
225 g (8 oz) carrots	4 drops Tabasco sauce
50 g (2 oz) pecan nuts or walnuts (optional)	salt and pepper
DRESSING	**TO GARNISH**
75 g (5 tbsp) mayonnaise	paprika, for sprinkling
30 ml (2 tbsp) olive oil	chervil or parsley sprigs

1 Fit the slicing disc, preferably a thick slicing disc. Remove the core from the cabbage, cut into large chunks to fit in the feed tube and shred. Slice the celery.

2 Fit the medium or coarse grating disc. Peel the carrots and grate. Combine the cabbage, celery and carrots in a large bowl.

3 Fit the metal blade, add the dressing ingredients and process for a few seconds, until well blended. Pour over the salad and toss well. Cover and leave to stand for several hours or overnight if possible, in a cool place.

4 Just before serving, toss the nuts into the salad. Sprinkle with a little paprika and garnish with chervil or parsley.

Artichoke and Spinach Salad

An interesting and tasty warm winter salad. Jerusalem artichokes are sliced, cooked and then marinated in garlic flavoured olive oil. They are quickly browned under the grill and tossed with young spinach leaves.

Preparation time: 15 minutes, plus marinating
Cooking time: 15-20 minutes
Cals per serving: 110

Serves 6

450 g (1 lb) Jerusalem artichokes	**1 garlic clove**
salt and pepper	**60 ml (4 tbsp) olive oil**
2 lemons	**175 g (6 oz) young spinach leaves**

1 Scrub the artichokes. Fit the slicing disc and slice the artichokes. Place in a large pan of boiling salted water. Add the grated rind and juice of 1 lemon. Simmer for about 5 minutes or until just tender.

2 Peel the garlic and crush. Whisk together the olive oil, garlic and juice from the remaining lemon. Season with salt and pepper.

3 Drain the artichokes, then toss in the dressing. Leave to cool, then cover and leave to stand for 1-2 hours.

4 Remove any tough stalks from the spinach; tear the leaves into small pieces if necessary.

5 Spoon the artichokes into a grill pan with any remaining marinade. Grill on both sides for 3-4 minutes until browned.

6 Gently toss the artichokes and any pan juices with the spinach. Adjust the seasoning and serve immediately.

Beetroot and Cucumber Salad

This sweet and sour salad is quick to make and has a delicious creamy dill dressing.
If uncooked beetroots are available, they will impart a better flavour, but for convenience you
can buy ready-cooked beetroots.

Preparation time: 20 minutes
Cooking time: Nil
Cals per serving: 360
Serves 6

1 medium cucumber	**small bunch fresh dill**
900 g (1½ lb) cooked beetroots	**5 ml (1 tsp) red wine vinegar**
4 pickled dill cucumbers	**squeeze of lemon juice**
6 spring onions	**salt and pepper**
DRESSING	**200 ml (7 fl oz) soured cream or crème fraîche**
150 ml (¼ pint) sunflower oil	**TO GARNISH**
1 egg	**dill sprigs**
45 ml (3 tbsp) Dijon mustard	

1 Fit the stir-fry or chipper disc. Cut the cucumber into 5 cm (2 inch) lengths and place horizontally in the feed tube. Cut into sticks, remove and set aside.

2 Peel the beetroots and cut in half, if large, to fit the feed tube. Using the stir-fry or chipper disc, cut into sticks. Arrange on a flat plate or in a shallow dish. Arrange the cucumber on top of the beetroot.

3 Dice the dill cucumbers and slice the spring onions. Scatter over the cucumber.

4 To make the dressing, place 45 ml (3 tbsp) sunflower oil in the food processor, fitted with the metal blade. Add the egg, mustard, dill, vinegar, lemon juice and salt and pepper. Blend for a few seconds, until evenly mixed and thickened.

5 With the processor running, pour in the rest of the oil in a thin steady stream. Stir in the soured cream or crème fraîche. Drizzle over the salad and garnish with dill sprigs to serve.

Fennel and Pear Salad

The slicing disc on the food processor will quickly prepare this side salad.

Preparation time: 10 minutes
Cooking time: Nil
Cals per serving: 140
Serves 6

2 bulbs Florence fennel	**black pepper**
2 firm ripe pears	**50 ml (2 fl oz) extra-virgin olive oil**

1 Remove the feathery tops from the fennel and roughly chop. Cut the bulbs in half lengthways. Quarter the pears and remove the cores.

2 Fit the slicing disc and slice the fennel. Arrange on a serving plate. Slice the pears lengthways and scatter over the fennel. Sprinkle with pepper and olive oil.

Greek Salad

Cucumber and tomato slices, green pepper, olives and feta, make this mouthwatering salad.

Preparation time: 10 minutes
Cooking time: Nil
Cals per serving: 525-350
Serves 4-6

700 g (1½ lb) firm tomatoes	**125 g (4 oz) black olives, pitted**
1 medium cucumber	**4-5 sprigs fresh oregano**
1 medium green pepper	**135 ml (9 tbsp) olive oil**
225 g (8 oz) feta cheese	**45 ml (3 tbsp) lemon juice**

1 Fit the thick or medium slicing disc. Slice the tomatoes and arrange in a serving bowl. Halve the cucumber lengthways and slice. Halve, core and deseed the pepper, then cut into strips. Dice the cheese. Add the cucumber, green pepper, cheese and olives to the salad.

2 Fit the metal blade. Place the oregano leaves in the food processor with the olive oil and lemon juice. Process for a few seconds, until emulsified. Pour over salad and toss gently. Serve at once.

Mixed Leaf Salad

This colourful salad combines a mixture of salad leaves, with finely shredded vegetables, tossed in an olive oil and balsamic vinegar dressing. It makes the perfect accompaniment to a main course fish or meat dish.

Preparation time: 20 minutes

Cooking time: Nil

Cals per serving: 285

Serves 6

½ cos lettuce	**DRESSING**
75 g (3 oz) mixed salad leaves such as lamb's lettuce, oak leaf lettuce and batavia	small bunch fresh parsley or dill
40 g (1½ oz) rocket leaves	175 ml (6 fl oz) extra-virgin olive oil
1 carrot	30 ml (2 tbsp) balsamic vinegar
1 courgette	5 ml (1 tsp) Dijon mustard
2 celery sticks	2.5 ml (½ tsp) sugar
1 small red onion	coarse sea salt and pepper
1 head chicory	**TO GARNISH**
½ head fennel	herb sprigs
225 g (8 oz) small cherry tomatoes	

1 Carefully wash all the salad ingredients and allow to drain in a colander. Tear the leaves into smaller pieces if necessary and place in a salad bowl.

2 Peel the carrot. Cut the carrot, courgette and celery into 6.5 cm (2½ inch) lengths. Fit the stir-fry or chipper disc and cut the vegetables into thin sticks. If the chipper disc makes large chips, use the very large 8mm grater disc instead.

3 Peel and quarter the onion. Halve the chicory lengthways. Fit the slicing disc, slice the onions and fennel and shred the chicory.

4 Add the carrot, courgette, celery, onion, fennel, chicory and tomatoes to the salad leaves and toss lightly.

5 To make the dressing, fit the metal blade and place all the dressing ingredients in the food processor. Process for 10-15 seconds or until the mixture has emulsified.

6 To serve, pour the dressing over the salad and toss lightly. Serve at once, garnished with herb sprigs.

Indonesian Salad

This mixed vegetable salad is served with a warm, slightly piquant peanut sauce.
It can be served as an accompaniment to a light main course or on its own as a main
course salad. Serves four as a main course salad.

Preparation time: 35 minutes
Cooking time: 20-25 minutes
Cals per serving: 330

Serves 6

125 g (4 oz) shallots	175 g (6 oz) cauliflower
1 garlic clove	125 g (4 oz) cabbage
15 ml (1 tbsp) sunflower oil	150 g (5 oz) cucumber
2.5 ml (½ tsp) chilli powder	175 g (6 oz) new potatoes
15 ml (1 tbsp) soft brown sugar	175 g (6 oz) baby carrots
125 g (4 oz) roasted, salted peanuts	175 g (6 oz) French beans
25 g (1 oz) creamed coconut	3 hard-boiled eggs
1 lemon	**TO SERVE**
salt and pepper	50 g (2 oz) prawn crackers, optional

1 Fit the metal blade. Peel the shallots and garlic, place in the food processor and finely chop. Heat the oil in a frying pan. Add the shallots and garlic to the pan and cook, stirring for 1 minute.

2 Add the chilli powder, sugar and 150 ml (¼ pint) water and bring to the boil. Place the peanuts in the food processor and process to a powder. Add to the saucepan and simmer for 5 minutes.

3 Fit the grating disc and grate the creamed coconut. Stir into the peanut mixture. Squeeze the juice of the lemon, stir into the dressing and cook for 1 minute. Adjust the seasoning and set aside.

4 Cut the cauliflower into florets. Fit the slicing blade, shred the cabbage and slice the cucumber.

5 Cook the potatoes in a pan of boiling lightly salted water until just tender. Drain and cool. Bring a large pan of salted water to the boil, add the cabbage, cauliflower, baby carrots and French beans and cook for 3 minutes. Drain, refresh in cold water and drain again.

6 Gently reheat the peanut sauce until just below boiling and pour over the vegetables; toss well. Peel and quarter the eggs. Arrange the vegetables on a platter with the eggs. Serve with prawn crackers, if desired.

Smoked Mussel and Pasta Salad

If time allows make this salad in advance, to give the flavours time to mingle, but add the avocado just before serving.

Preparation time: 15 minutes
Cooking time: 15-20 minutes
Cals per serving: 660
Serves 4

2 medium red peppers	salt and pepper
8 salad onions	350 g (12 oz) dried pasta shells
90 ml (3 fl oz) olive oil	125 g (4 oz) fresh or frozen peas
small bunch fresh parsley	1 medium avocado
1 garlic clove	two 105 g (3½ oz) cans smoked mussels, drained
10 ml (2 tsp) red wine vinegar	

1 Cut the peppers into quarters, then remove the core and seeds. Peel the onions and cut into quarters.

2 Preheat the grill. Place the quartered onions and peppers, skin side up, in the grill pan and drizzle with 15 ml (1 tbsp) of the olive oil. Grill until the pepper skins are charred and the onions are nicely browned. You may need to remove the onions before the peppers.

3 Place the peppers in a bowl, cover with a plate; the steam created will help to loosen the skins. When the peppers are cool enough to handle, peel away the skins.

4 Fit the metal blade. Finely chop the parsley and set aside. Place half the peppers in the food processor. Peel the garlic and add with the remaining oil and vinegar. Process to a purée, and season with salt and pepper, to taste.

5 Cook the pasta in a large pan of boiling salted water until 'al dente' or according to the packet instructions. About 5 minutes before the end of the cooking time, add the peas. Drain the cooked pasta and peas, then immediately refresh under cold running water. Drain thoroughly.

6 Cut the remaining pepper into strips. Halve the avocado, remove the stone and skin, then cut into chunks.

7 Transfer the pasta and peas to a large bowl, add the pepper strips, grilled onions, mussels, 45 ml (3 tbsp) chopped parsley and avocado. Toss gently to combine all the ingredients and check the seasoning. Serve sprinkled with the remaining chopped parsley.

NOTE: Canned smoked mussels are available from large supermarkets and delicatessens. Smoked oysters are a delicious alternative.

DESSERTS

Lemon and Raspberry Puffs

A light and fluffy lemon soufflé, sits atop a layer of raspberries for this hot summer dessert.

Preparation time: 15 minutes
Cooking time: 15 minutes
Cals per serving: 170
Serves 6

about 50 g (2 oz) butter	**2 eggs**
125 g (4 oz) raspberries	**25 g (1 oz) caster sugar**
30 ml (2 tbsp) icing sugar	**1 lemon**
25 g (1 oz) plain white flour	**icing sugar, for dusting**
200 ml (7 fl oz) milk	

1 Preheat the oven to 190°C (375°F) Mark 5. Lightly grease six 150 ml (¼ pint) ramekin dishes with a little butter. Gently toss the raspberries and icing sugar together and divide between the ramekin dishes.

2 Fit the metal blade. Place 40 g (1½ oz) butter and the flour in the food processor. Process until blended. Pour the milk into a saucepan and bring to the boil. Pour into the food processor and mix, using a pulse action, until smooth. Return to the saucepan and bring to the boil, stirring. Cool slightly.

3 Separate the eggs and beat the egg yolks and then the caster sugar into the sauce. Grate the lemon rind and add with 15 ml (1 tbsp) lemon juice. Mix thoroughly to combine.

4 Using the cleaned food processor bowl, fit the whisk, add the egg whites and whisk until stiff. Using a large metal spoon, beat one small spoonful of egg white into the sauce to lighten it, then carefully fold in the remainder.

5 Spoon the mixture into the prepared dishes and place on a baking sheet. Bake for 15-20 minutes, or until lightly set. Dust the tops with icing sugar and serve immediately.

Mascarpone and Pear Tranche

This gorgeous, rich and creamy fruit tart is served with a lemony pear sauce.

Preparation time: 30 minutes
Cooking time: 55-60 minutes
Cals per serving: 740-555
Serves 6-8

65 g (2½ oz) unsalted butter	**2 eggs**
150 g (5 oz) plain white flour	**15 ml (1 tbsp) rum**
50 g (2 oz) caster sugar	**1.25 ml (¼ tsp) vanilla essence**
FILLING	**25 g (1 oz) caster sugar**
225 g (8 oz) pears	**30 ml (2 tbsp) soft dark brown sugar**
1 banana	**PEAR SAUCE**
175 g (6 oz) fresh dates	**50 g (2 oz) caster sugar**
25 g (1 oz) butter	**1 lemon**
175 g (6 oz) mascarpone cheese	**225 g (8 oz) ripe pears**

1 Fit the metal blade. Dice the butter and process with the flour until it resembles fine breadcrumbs. Add the sugar and process for a few seconds to mix. Sprinkle on 30 ml (2 tbsp) cold water and process until the pastry clings together. Wrap and chill for 30 minutes.

2 Preheat the oven to 200°C (400°F) Mark 6. Roll out the dough on a lightly floured surface and use to line a 34 x 11.5 cm (13½ x 4½ inch) loose-based, fluted tranche tin. Prick the base, line with greaseproof paper and baking beans and bake blind for 15-20 minutes, removing the paper and beans for the last 5 minutes.

3 Peel, quarter and core the pears. Slice the banana. Halve and stone the dates. Melt the butter in a large, heavy-based sauté pan, stir in the pears and dates and sauté for 3-4 minutes, until beginning to soften. Add the banana and cook for 1 minute.

4 Arrange the fruit in the pastry case. Using the metal blade blend the cheese, eggs, rum, vanilla and caster sugar together for a few seconds, until smooth. Spoon over the fruit to cover. Sprinkle with a little brown sugar.

5 Reduce the oven to 170°C (325°F) Mark 3. Bake the tart for about 35 minutes, or until set. Sprinkle with a little more brown sugar and flash under a preheated grill to caramelise the sugar.

6 Make the pear sauce. Dissolve the sugar in 175ml (6 fl oz) water over a gentle heat. Grate the lemon rind. Peel, quarter, core and chop the pears. Add to the pan with the lemon rind and bring to the boil. Simmer for 5 minutes, or until softened. Using the metal blade, process to a purée. Stir in 15 ml (1 tbsp) lemon juice and sieve. Serve the tart warm, with the pear sauce.

Walnut and Fig Tart

This delicious tart has moist sticky figs mixed into a dark treacly filling, with walnuts added to give a nutty crunch. Serve warm with crème fraîche or ice-cream.

Preparation time: 50 minutes, plus cooling
Cooking time: 40-45 minutes
Cals per serving:470
Serves 8

175 g (6 oz) plain white flour	**100 g (3½ oz) crustless white bread**
pinch of salt	**90 ml (6 tbsp) molasses or dark treacle**
125 g (4 oz) butter	**135 ml (9 tbsp) golden syrup**
2 egg yolks	**30 ml (2 tbsp) lemon juice**
FILLING	**125 g (4 oz) shelled walnuts**
150 g (5 oz) ready-to-eat dried figs	

1 Fit the metal blade. Place the flour and salt in the food processor. Dice the butter and add to the processor bowl. Blend until the mixture resembles fine breadcrumbs.

2 Add the egg yolks and process until the mixture binds together, adding a little cold water if necessary. Wrap the pastry and chill for 30 minutes.

3 Preheat the oven to 200°C (400°F) Mark 6. Roll out the pastry on a lightly floured surface and use to line a 23 cm (9 inch) round loose-based fluted flan tin. Prick the base with a fork and chill for 10 minutes.

4 Place on a baking sheet and line the pastry case with greaseproof paper and baking beans. Bake blind for 15 minutes. Remove the paper and beans and bake for 5 minutes.

5 Meanwhile trim the stems from the figs and cut into small chunks. Set aside. Tear the bread into pieces and using the metal blade process into breadcrumbs.

6 Add the molasses or treacle, golden syrup and lemon juice and process briefly until just combined. Add 75 g (3 oz) walnuts and process for a few seconds until they are cut into rough chunks.

7 Scatter the figs over the cooked pastry case. Spread the breadcrumb filling on top. Arrange the remaining walnuts on top and press them down gently. Bake for 20-25 minutes until the filling is just firm.

8 Leave to cool on a wire rack until warm before serving. Serve with crème fraîche or ice cream, if desired.

Cherry Streusel Slice

Reminiscent of a traditional fruit crumble, this dessert has a generous filling of cherries inside a buttery, almond crumble shell. Serve sliced, with spoonfuls of whipped cream or crème fraîche.

Preparation time: 20 minutes, plus cooling
Cooking time: 40-45 minutes
Cals per serving: 480
Serves 8

two 425 g (15 oz) cans pitted black or red cherries	grated rind ½ lemon
10 ml (2 tsp) cornflour	165 g (5½ oz) caster sugar
5 ml (1 tsp) vanilla essence	50 g (2 oz) ground almonds
175 g (6 oz) unsalted butter	1 egg
250 g (9 oz) self-raising white flour	icing sugar, for dusting
5 ml (1 tsp) ground cinnamon	

1 Drain the cherries, reserving 90 ml (3 fl oz) of the juice. Blend a little of the juice with the cornflour in a small pan. Add the remaining juice and vanilla essence and bring to the boil, stirring. Add the cherries and cook, stirring, for a further 1 minute until thickly coated in syrup.

2 Grease a 1.4 litre (2½ pint) loaf tin. Line the base and long sides with a double thickness of greaseproof paper, allowing it to overhang the sides of the tin. Preheat the oven to 180°C (350°F) Mark 4.

3 Fit the food processor with the metal blade. Cut the butter into small pieces and place in the food processor bowl with the flour, cinnamon and lemon rind. Process until the mixture starts to cling together. Add the sugar and ground almonds, and process briefly until the mixture resembles a coarse crumble.

4 Weigh 150 g (5 oz) of the crumble and set aside for the topping. Add the egg to the remaining mixture and process to a fairly soft paste. Use half to thickly line the base of the tin. Roll out the remainder and cut into strips about 2.5 cm (1 inch) wide. Use these to line the sides of the tin, pressing them to fit around the corners and base, eliminating the joins.

5 Spoon the cherry filling into the centre and sprinkle evenly with the reserved crumble. Bake for 40-45 minutes until the topping is pale golden. Leave in the tin to cool until just warm.

6 Loosen the edges at the ends of the tin, then carefully lift out the dessert, using the greaseproof paper. Serve warm, dusted with icing sugar.

Heavenly Cheesecake

This cheesecake tastes delicious served warm or cold. The heavenly flavour comes from a combination of lemon and ginger. Serve warm with a selection of fresh berry fruits for a summertime dessert.

Preparation time: 20 minutes, plus cooling
Cooking time: 50-55 minutes
Cals per serving: 345
Serves 6

175 g (6 oz) digestive biscuits	**125 g (4 oz) caster sugar**
25 g (1 oz) butter, melted	**60 ml (4 tbsp) crème fraîche**
50 g (2 oz) stem ginger	**1 egg**
400 g (14 oz) full fat soft cheese	**icing sugar, for dusting**
1 large or 2 small lemons	

1 Preheat the oven to 180°C (350°F) Mark 4. Line the base of an 18 cm (7 inch) base measurement, spring-release cake tin with non-stick baking parchment.

2 Fit the metal blade. Add the digestive biscuits, butter and ginger and process until the biscuits form a crumb, ginger is finely chopped and the ingredients are combined. Press into the base of the tin and bake for 15 minutes or until just beginning to change colour.

3 Place the cheese in the cleaned food processor bowl. Finely grate the lemon rind and add with 60 ml (4 tbsp) of lemon juice. Add the sugar, crème fraîche and egg and process briefly until thoroughly mixed and smooth. Spoon onto the warm biscuit base. Bake for 35-40 minutes, or until just set.

4 Cool in the tin for 30 minutes. Loosen the edges of the cheesecake then remove the sides of the tin. Leave on the tin base and serve warm, generously dusted with icing sugar.

Chocolate Blinis with Caramel

A buttery, hazelnut and caramel sauce, is poured over these chocolate blinis, which are oozing with chocolate; a dessert which is impossible to resist.

Preparation time: 15 minutes
Cooking time: 20 minutes
Cals per serving: 350
Serves 6

75 g (3 oz) milk chocolate	**a little oil, for cooking**
100 g (3½ oz) self-raising white flour	**SAUCE**
15 g (½ oz) cocoa powder	**50 g (2 oz) shelled hazelnuts**
2.5 ml (½ tsp) baking powder	**75 g (3 oz) caster sugar**
15 ml (1 tbsp) caster sugar	**grated rind ½ orange**
1 egg	**40 g (1½ oz) unsalted butter**
200 ml (7 fl oz) milk	

1 Fit the metal blade. Break the chocolate into pieces, place in the food processor and using pulse setting roughly chop the chocolate. Set aside.

2 Add the flour, cocoa powder, baking powder and sugar to the food processor. Process for a few seconds to mix. Add the egg and half the milk and process until combined. Gradually add the remaining milk and mix to a thick batter. Pour into a jug and leave to stand while making the sauce.

3 Roughly chop the hazelnuts. Preheat the grill, then toast the nuts, turning frequently, until evenly golden.

4 Put the sugar in a small heavy-based saucepan with 90 ml (3 fl oz) water and heat gently until the sugar dissolves. Bring to the boil and boil rapidly until deep golden. Immerse the base of the pan in cold water to prevent further cooking.

5 Carefully add 30 ml (2 tbsp) cold water, standing back, as the syrup will splutter. Add the hazelnuts, orange rind and butter, and reheat gently until smooth and glossy.

6 Cook the blinis in batches. Heat a little oil in a large frying pan or griddle over a moderate heat. Add dessertspoonfuls of the batter, spacing them well apart. Fry gently for 2 minutes or until bubbles appear on the surface. Flip the blinis over with a palette knife and cook until just firm. Transfer to a warmed plate.

7 Gently reheat the sauce. Transfer the blinis to serving plates, allowing three each, and pour a little of the sauce over them. Serve immediately.

Crispy Apple Clafoutis

A cinnamon and armagnac flavoured batter envelopes layers of apple slices in this mouthwatering dessert. The top cooks to a crispy finish and is served, dusted with sugar.

Preparation time: 15 minutes, plus standing

Cooking time: 45-50 minutes

Calories per serving: 270

Serves 6

50 g (2 oz) self-raising white flour	30 ml (2 tbsp) armagnac
150 g (5 oz) plain white flour	50 g (2 oz) butter
large pinch of salt	350 g (12 oz) ripe dessert apples
5 ml (1 tsp) ground cinnamon	**TO SERVE**
50 g (2 oz) caster sugar	caster sugar, for dusting
3 eggs	icing sugar, for dusting
200 ml (7 fl oz) milk	

1 Fit the metal blade. Add the flours, salt, ground cinnamon and sugar and process for a few seconds to mix the dry ingredients. Add the eggs and half the milk and process until combined and the mixture is smooth.

2 Add the remaining milk and armagnac and mix to a batter. Pour into a large jug, cover and leave to stand for 2 hours.

3 Using half the butter, grease a 23 cm (9 inch) spring-release cake tin. Stand it on a baking sheet. Fit the medium or thick slicing disc. Halve and core the apples and then slice.

4 Preheat the oven to 220°C (425°F) Mark 7. Stir the batter and pour into the prepared tin and lay the fruit slices on top. Dot with the remaining butter. Bake for 45-50 minutes, or until risen and well browned.

5 Dust with a mixture of caster sugar and icing sugar. Remove the cake tin sides and place the clafoutis on a serving plate.

Cranberry and Orange Mousse

This interesting combination of cranberries and orange gives a refreshing flavour to the creamy mousse base. A perfect dessert for the festive season. Use frozen cranberries when fresh cranberries are out of season.

Preparation time: 30 minutes, plus chilling
Cooking time: 10 minutes
Cals per serving: 300
Serves 6

300 g (11 oz) fresh cranberries	**finely grated rind 1 orange**
150 ml (¼ pint) orange juice	**300 ml (½ pint) double cream**
75 g (3 oz) caster sugar	**2 egg whites**
30 ml (2 tbsp) Cointreau or other orange liqueur	**TO DECORATE**
15 ml (1 tbsp) powdered gelatine	**grated orange rind**
3 egg yolks	

1 Place the cranberries, orange juice and 25 g (1 oz) sugar in a saucepan. Bring to a gentle boil then simmer for 5-6 minutes, or until the berries start to pop.

2 Remove from the heat and leave to cool for 5 minutes. Fit the food processor with the metal blade, add the cranberry mixture and purée. Pass through a sieve to remove the pips. Set aside until cold. Stir in the Cointreau.

3 In a small bowl sprinkle the gelatine over 45 ml (3 tbsp) water and leave to soak for 2-3 minutes. Place the bowl over a pan of simmering water until the gelatine dissolves.

4 Place the egg yolks, orange rind and remaining sugar in a large bowl and whisk together until pale and creamy. Fit the food processor with the whisk attachment and whisk the cream until it forms soft peaks.

5 Stir the gelatine into the whisked egg yolk mixture, then stir in the fruit purée. Fold in the cream and chill until the mixture is on the point of setting.

6 Using a cleaned food processor bowl and whisk attachment, add the egg whites and whisk for about 1 minute, until stiff. Fold into the mousse. Pour into a serving dish and chill for 1 hour, to completely set. Sprinkle with grated orange rind and serve.

Coconut Bavarois

A creamy moulded custard, flavoured with coconut and vanilla, served with a tropical fruit sauce.

Preparation time: 30 minutes, plus chilling
Cooking time: 15 minutes
Cals per serving: 500
Serves: 6

400 ml (14 fl oz) can coconut milk	**SAUCE**
200 ml (7 fl oz) milk	**1 large ripe mango, about 450 g (1 lb)**
4 egg yolks	**juice 1 large orange**
125 g (4 oz) caster sugar	**juice 1 lime**
2.5 ml (½ tsp) vanilla essence	**2 ripe passion fruits**
25 ml (5 tsp) powdered gelatine	**icing sugar, to taste**
30-45 ml (2-3 tbsp) coconut liqueur	**TO DECORATE**
150 ml (¼ pint) double cream	**mint sprigs**
	finely shredded orange and lemon rinds

1 Lightly oil six 150 ml (¼ pint) individual moulds. Pour the coconut milk into a non-aluminium saucepan. Add the milk and mix together. Heat gently until almost boiling.

2 Fit the metal blade. Place the egg yolks and sugar in the food processor. With the machine running add the milk down the feed tube. Return the sauce to the pan and cook over a gentle heat, stirring continuously until slightly thickened. Do not boil or it will curdle.

3 Strain into a bowl, stir in the vanilla essence and cover with damp greaseproof paper to prevent a skin forming. Leave to cool. Put 50 ml (2 fl oz) cold water in a small bowl and sprinkle on the gelatine. Leave until softened then stand in a pan of simmering water and stir occasionally until dissolved. Stir into the cold custard with the coconut liqueur. Chill until it begins to thicken.

4 Fit the whisk attachment and whip the cream until it forms soft peaks, then fold into the custard. Spoon into the moulds, cover and chill for at least 2-3 hours until set.

5 To make the sauce, peel and stone the mango. Chop the flesh and place in the food processor, fitted with the metal blade. Add the orange and lime juice and purée until smooth. Pass through a sieve into a bowl. Halve the passion fruit and scoop out the seeds into the mango sauce. If the sauce is too thick stir in a little more orange juice. Stir in icing sugar, to taste.

6 To serve, run a thin-bladed knife around each bavarois and invert onto a dessert plate. Spoon over a little sauce and pour the rest around the bavarois. Decorate with mint and shredded orange and lime rind.

Chocolate Marquise

To make this dessert a very rich chocolate mousse is poured over a crisp chocolate biscuit base and then chilled until set. Make sure the refrigerator is very cold otherwise the mousse will not be firm enough to slice. Alternatively place in the freezer for 30 minutes, before serving.

Preparation time: 25 minutes, plus chilling
Cooking time: Nil
Cals per serving: 485-390
Serves 8-10

BISCUIT BASE	45 ml (3 tbsp) strong black coffee
175 g (6 oz) or chocolate wholemeal biscuits	50 g (2 oz) unsalted butter
65 g (2½ oz) butter	4 eggs
CHOCOLATE MOUSSE	125 g (4 oz) caster sugar
5 ml (1 tsp) powdered gelatine	TO DECORATE
15 ml (1 tbsp) whisky	white chocolate curls
200 g (7 oz) plain chocolate	45 ml (3 tbsp) cocoa powder

1 Grease and line a 23 cm (9 inch) spring-release round cake tin. Fit the metal blade, add the biscuits and process briefly to a coarse crumb. Melt the butter in a saucepan and stir in the biscuit crumbs. Spoon into the prepared tin and press into an even layer. Set aside.

2 Sprinkle the gelatine over the whisky in a small bowl. Stand in a pan of hot water and stir to dissolve. To make the mousse topping, break the chocolate into small pieces and place in a heatproof bowl with the coffee, butter and dissolved gelatine. Place the bowl over a pan of hot water and leave to melt.

3 Separate the eggs and place the yolks and sugar in a large bowl over a pan of simmering water. Whisk, using an electric beater or balloon whisk, until the mixture is thick and foamy and will hold a trail from the whisk.

4 Using the cleaned food processor bowl, fit the whisk and whisk the egg whites for about 2 minutes, until they hold soft peaks. Leave the pusher out of the feed tube to allow air to circulate.

5 Fold the chocolate mixture into the whisked egg yolk mixture, then stir in one third of the egg whites. Fold in the rest and pour into the prepared tin. Spread evenly, then cover and chill in the refrigerator overnight.

6 To serve, unclip the spring-release tin and peel away the lining paper. Carefully transfer the marquise to a serving plate and decorate with with chocolate curls. Dust liberally with cocoa powder and serve.

Chocolate and Banana Creams

Creamy yogurt and white chocolate, flavoured with banana purée are layered together to make this mouthwatering dessert. Each layer is scattered with dark muscovado sugar. Allow at least an hour before serving, for the sugar to turn syrupy.

Preparation time: 15 minutes, plus chilling
Cooking time: Nil
Cals per serving: 585
Serves 4

175 g (6 oz) white chocolate	**250 g (9 oz) Greek-style yogurt**
150 ml (¼ pint) double cream	**40 g (1½ oz) dark muscovado sugar**
2 ripe bananas	**TO DECORATE**
20 ml (4 tsp) lemon juice	**chocolate curls**

1 Break up the chocolate and put in a heatproof bowl set over a pan of simmering water. Add 45 ml (3 tbsp) of the cream and leave until melted.

2 Mash the bananas in a bowl, using a fork, then mix in the lemon juice. Fit the metal blade. Transfer the banana to the food processor, add the melted chocolate mixture and process briefly until smooth. Transfer to a bowl and chill for about 1 hour until firmer in texture.

3 Fit the whisk attachment and lightly whip the remaining cream for a few seconds, until it just begins to hold its shape. Add the yogurt and mix briefly to combine. Spoon a third of this mixture into the bases of 4 stemmed serving glasses. Sprinkle with a little muscovado sugar.

4 Spoon half the banana mixture over the cream and sprinkle with a little more of the sugar. Add another cream layer, then the remaining banana mixture and finally the remaining cream, sprinkling each layer with the sugar. Keep in a cool place until required.

5 Scatter a few chocolate curls on top of each dessert just before serving.

Lemon Fudge Tart

An easy to make lemon dessert. A buttery, yet tangy lemon filling on a crumbly shortbread base. It can be made up to 2 days in advance and kept in an airtight container in the refrigerator until needed.

Preparation time: 20 minutes, plus chilling
Cooking time: 1¼-1½ hours
Cals per serving: 295
Serves 8

50 g (2 oz) butter	**5 eggs**
100 g (4 oz) plain white flour	**150 g (5 oz) caster sugar**
15 ml (1 tbsp) icing sugar	**TO DECORATE**
FILLING	**icing sugar**
75 g (3 oz) butter	**few fresh strawberries or strands of redcurrants**
3 lemons	

1 Preheat the oven to 170°C (325°F) Mark 3. Fit the metal blade. Cut the butter into pieces. Place in the food processor with the flour and icing sugar and process until the mixture resembles breadcrumbs.

2 Transfer to a 22 cm (8½ inch) ceramic flan dish and press over the base using your fingertips. Bake for 35-40 minutes, until golden.

3 Meanwhile make the filling. Melt the butter in a small saucepan. Grate the rind from 1 lemon. Halve the lemons and squeeze the juice, using the citrus press. Measure 200 ml (7 fl oz) lemon juice.

4 Fit the metal blade, place the melted butter, lemon rind, lemon juice, eggs and caster sugar in the food processor and process until smooth. Pour over the warm shortbread. The shortbread base must be warm, or the crumbs will rise to the surface.

5 Reduce the oven to 130°C (250°F) Mark ½. Bake for 45-50 minutes, or until just set. Leave to cool then refrigerate until ready to serve.

6 To serve, remove from the refrigerator for 1 hour. Cut into wedges and ease out of the dish. Arrange on a serving plate and dust heavily with icing sugar. Decorate with fresh fruit and serve.

Minted Blueberry Meringue

The simple combination of a light meringue, cream and fruit makes an ever popular dessert.
This swirled meringue is topped with whipped cream and plenty of fresh blueberries.

Preparation time: 20 minutes, plus cooling
Cooking time: About 2 hours
Cals per serving: 310

Serves 6

	TO DECORATE
4 egg whites	**fresh mint sprigs**
175 g (6 oz) caster sugar	**caster sugar, for dusting**
450 ml (¾ pint) double cream	
175 g (6 oz) fresh blueberries	

1 Mark a 23 x 12 cm (9 x 5 inch) rectangle on a sheet of non-stick baking parchment. Place on a baking sheet. Preheat oven to 100°C (200°F) Mark low.

2 Fit the food processor with the whisk attachment. Leave the pusher out of the feed tube. Add the egg whites and half the sugar and whisk for about 1½ minutes, until stiff. Gradually add the remaining sugar, 1 tablespoonful at a time, whisking for 10 seconds in between each addition.

3 Spoon the meringue onto the rectangle and spread into the corners. Peak the meringue with the back of a spoon.

4 Bake for 1¾-2 hours, until very crisp. Leave to cool on the paper.

5 Using the whisk attachment, whip the cream until it forms soft peaks. Spoon on top of the meringue. Scatter over the blueberries. To decorate, arrange mint sprigs casually over the top and dust the mint and fruit with caster sugar.

Rhubarb Parfait

Rhubarb and orange complement each other beautifully in this frozen dessert. Serve with crisp dessert biscuits.

Preparation time: 40 minutes, plus freezing
Cooking time: About 20 minutes
Cals per serving: 225

Serves 8

200 ml (7 fl oz) milk	**30 ml (2 tsp) orange juice**
finely pared rind 1 orange	**250 ml (8 fl oz) double cream**
4 egg yolks	**TO SERVE**
150 g (5 oz) caster sugar	**150 ml (¼ pint) crème fraîche or**
450 g (1 lb) rhubarb	**Greek-style yogurt**

1 Line a 1 litre (1¾ pint) loaf tin with cling film. Pour the milk into a saucepan, add the orange rind and slowly bring to the boil over a very low heat.

2 Meanwhile, fit the metal blade, place the egg yolks and sugar in the food processor and process for a few seconds to mix. Add the milk and process until blended. Strain back into the saucepan.

3 Cook the custard over a very low heat, stirring constantly, until it thickens enough to coat the back of a spoon; do not boil. Remove from the heat, pour into a large bowl and cool. Cover with dampened greaseproof paper to prevent a skin forming. Leave until cold.

4 Trim the rhubarb stalks then cut into short lengths and place in a saucepan with the orange juice. Cover and cook over a low heat for 5-7 minutes until the rhubarb is soft.

5 Place in the cleaned food processor bowl, fitted with the metal blade and process to a smooth purée. Transfer to a bowl and leave to cool.

6 When both the rhubarb and custard are cold, fit the whisk attachment and whip the cream until it holds soft peaks. Fold into the rhubarb with the custard. Pour into the prepared loaf tin. Cover with cling film and freeze for at least 6 hours, or overnight.

7 About 20 minutes before serving, transfer the rhubarb parfait to the refrigerator to soften slightly. Turn the rhubarb parfait out onto a cling film lined board. Cut into slices and arrange on serving plates. Serve at once, with a spoonful of crème fraîche or yogurt.

Mango, Ginger and Citrus Sorbet

This mango sorbet is flavoured with lime and stem ginger. The lime adds a refreshing tangy note to the flavour.

Preparation time: 25 minutes, plus freezing

Cooking time: 3-4 minutes

Cals per serving: 150-100

Serves 4-6

2 large mangoes, each about 400 g (14 oz)	**50 g (2 oz) caster sugar**
25 g (1 oz) preserved stem ginger	**finely grated rind and juice of 3 limes**
50 ml (2 fl oz) syrup from the stem ginger jar	

1 Peel the mangoes, using a potato peeler, then cut down either side of the central stone; cut away as much of the remaining flesh as possible. Chop the flesh. Fit the metal blade. Place the mango flesh in the food processor bowl and process to a purée.

2 Finely chop the stem ginger. Transfer the mango purée to a bowl, stir in the chopped ginger and set aside.

3 Place the ginger syrup in a small pan with the sugar, lime rind and juice and add 90 ml (3 fl oz) water. Heat gently until the sugar is dissolved stirring occasionally. Bring to the boil and simmer for 3 minutes. Remove from the heat and leave to cool.

4 Strain the cooled syrup through a fine sieve into the puréed mango mixture and stir well. Transfer to a plastic container and freeze for 2 hours.

5 Remove from the freezer and beat well to break down any ice crystals that may have formed. Return to the freezer for a further 1 hour, then beat again. Repeat once more. Freeze for several hours until firm, or until required.

6 Transfer the sorbet to the refrigerator about 20 minutes before serving to soften slightly. Scoop into individual glass dishes to serve.

BAKING

Carrot Cake

This carrot cake has a creamy mascarpone frosting, topped with crispy fried carrot shavings.

Preparation time: 25 minutes, plus cooling

Cooking time: 35-40 minutes

Cals per slice: 735-570

Makes 8-10 slices

125 g (4 oz) Brazil nuts	**50 g (2 oz) ground almonds**
350 g (12 oz) carrots	**FROSTING**
225 g (8 oz) unsalted butter, softened	**250 g (9 oz) mascarpone or low-fat cream cheese**
225 g (8 oz) caster sugar	**5 ml (1 tsp) finely grated orange rind**
175 g (6 oz) self-raising white flour	**30 ml (2 tbsp) orange juice**
5 ml (1 tsp) baking powder	**30 ml (2 tbsp) icing sugar**
2.5 ml (½ tsp) ground allspice	**TO DECORATE**
4 eggs	**1 large carrot**
grated rind of 1 orange	**oil, for frying**
15 ml (1 tbsp) orange juice	**icing sugar, for dusting**

1 Preheat the oven to 180°C (350°F) Mark 4. Grease and base-line two 18 cm (7 inch) base measurement moule à manque tins or sandwich tins. Dust the sides of the tins with flour and shake out the excess. Roughly chop the Brazil nuts and lightly toast them.

2 Fit the grating disc. Peel and finely grate the carrots. Transfer to a large bowl. Fit the metal blade. Dice the butter and place in the processor with the sugar, flour, baking powder, allspice, eggs, orange rind, juice and almonds. Process for about 15 seconds, or until smooth.

3 Transfer the mixture into the bowl with the carrots and fold in with the toasted nuts. Divide between the tins and level the surfaces. Bake for 35-40 minutes until risen and firm to the touch. Transfer to a wire rack to cool.

4 For the frosting, place all the ingredients in the food processor and briefly process, until blended. Use half to sandwich the cakes together. Spread the remainder over the top of the cake, swirling it attractively.

5 For the decoration, peel the carrot and pare into long thin ribbons, using a swivel vegetable peeler. Dry the carrot ribbons on absorbent kitchen paper.

6 Heat 1 cm (½ inch) depth of oil in a frying pan until a piece of carrot added to the hot oil sizzles on the surface. Fry the carrots, in two batches, until golden. Drain and dry on kitchen paper. Scatter over the cake and dust with icing sugar. Chill until ready to serve.

NOTE Use a coarse grating disc to grate the carrots, for a lighter cake.

Spiced Apple and Almond Cake

This moist, spicy cake conceals a layer of apple through the centre.

Preparation time: 15 minutes, plus cooling

Cooking time: 1 hour

Cals per slice: 165

Makes 25 slices

700 g (1½ lb) crisp eating apples	**4 eggs, size 2**
15 ml (1 tbsp) lemon juice	**2.5 ml (½ tsp) almond essence**
225 g (8 oz) self-raising white flour	**25 g (1 oz) ground almonds**
10 ml (2 tsp) baking powder	**7.5 ml (1½ tsp) ground cinnamon**
225 g (8 oz) light soft brown sugar	

1 Grease and base-line a 5 cm (2 inch) deep, 20.5 cm (8 inch) square cake tin. Peel, quarter, core and roughly chop the apples and place in a saucepan. Add the lemon juice and 60 ml (4 tbsp) water. Cook over a gentle heat, until just beginning to soften and the liquid has evaporated. Leave to cool.

2 Preheat the oven to 180°C (350°F) Mark 4. Fit the metal blade. Put the flour, baking powder, sugar, eggs, almond essence, ground almonds and ground cinnamon in the food processor bowl. Add half the apple mixture and process for about 15 seconds, until blended and smooth.

3 Pour half the cake mixture into the prepared tin, spoon the remaining apples on top and level. Top with the remaining cake mixture to enclose all the apples.

4 Bake for about 1 hour. Cool in the tin for 5 minutes, before turning out onto a wire rack. Remove the paper and allow to cool. Store in an airtight container for up to 3 days.

Orange Sandwich Cake

A simple variation on a Victoria sandwich cake. Flavoured with orange and sandwiched with mascarpone and marmalade, this short-cut version tastes just as good as a traditionally made sponge.

Preparation time: 25 minutes, plus cooling
Cooking time: 25 minutes
Cals per serving: 420
Makes 12 slices

225 g (8 oz) unsalted butter, softened	**30 ml (2 tbsp) double cream**
225 g (8 oz) caster sugar	**60 ml (4 tbsp) thick shred orange marmalade**
4 eggs	**15 ml (1 tbsp) lemon juice**
225 g (8 oz) self-raising white flour	**30 ml (2 tbsp) orange flavoured liqueur (optional)**
5 ml (1 tsp) baking powder	**to decorate**
finely grated rind of 1 orange	**icing sugar, for dusting**
FILLING	
250 g (9 oz) mascarpone cheese	

1 Preheat the oven to 180°C (350°C) Mark 4. Grease and base-line two 20.5 cm (8 inch) sandwich tins.

2 Fit the metal blade. Cut the butter into pieces and place in the food processor with the sugar, eggs, flour, baking powder and orange rind. Process for about 30 seconds, or until smooth, scraping the mixture from the sides of the bowl if necessary after 15 seconds.

3 Divide the mixture between the prepared tins and level the surface. Bake for 25 minutes until well risen, firm to the touch and beginning to shrink from the sides of the tin. Turn out onto a wire rack and leave to cool.

4 Blend together the mascarpone cheese, cream, marmalade, lemon juice and liqueur, if using. Use to sandwich the two cakes together. Dust the top generously with icing sugar and serve.

VARIATIONS

For lemon or lime sandwich cakes, use grated lemon or lime rind in the cake and use the same flavoured marmalade in the filling.

Moist Ginger and Fruit Teabread

This teabread is packed with a mixture of dried fruits plumped up in black tea to produce a lovely moist texture. It will keep for several days, ready for slicing and serving on its own or buttered.

Preparation time: 10 minutes, plus soaking and cooling

Cooking time: 1¼ hours

Cals per serving: 185

Makes 12 slices

125 g (4 oz) dried apricots	**10 ml (2 tsp) baking powder**
125 g (4 oz) dried apples or pears	**125 g (4 oz) dark muscovado sugar**
125 g (4 oz) pitted dried prunes	**50 g (2 oz) caster sugar**
300 ml (½ pint) strong hot tea	**1 egg**
25 g (1 oz) stem ginger	**TO DECORATE**
225 g (8 oz) plain white flour	**caster sugar, for dusting**

1 Fit the metal blade. Add the dried apricots, apples and prunes and process briefly until the fruits are coarsely chopped. Transfer to a bowl and add the tea. Cover and leave for 2-3 hours until the liquid is completely absorbed.

2 Preheat the oven to 180°C (350°F) Mark 4. Grease the base and sides of a 1.1 litre (2 pint) loaf tin.

3 Chop the ginger into small pieces. Using the metal blade, briefly process the flour, baking powder, muscovado sugar, caster sugar and ginger to combine the ingredients.

4 Add the egg and steeped fruits and blend again until just mixed. Turn into the prepared tin and level the surface. Bake for 1¼ hours or until firm and a skewer inserted into the centre comes out clean.

5 Loosen the edges and turn out onto a wire rack to cool. Lightly dust with caster sugar and wrap in aluminium foil to store.

Zesty Lemon Curd Cakes

Bake these mouthwatering lemon flavoured cakes in individual cases or in one large tin.

Preparation time: 20 minutes, plus cooling
Cooking time: 20 minutes
Cals per cake: 250-220
Makes 12-14

175 g (6 oz) butter, softened	**1 lemon**
175 g (6 oz) caster sugar	**75 ml (5 tbsp) lemon curd**
225 g (8 oz) self-raising white flour	**TO SERVE**
5 ml (1 tsp) baking powder	**icing sugar, for dusting**
3 eggs	

1 Put 12-14 deep muffin cases into deep muffin tins or on a baking sheet, or line the base and sides of a 20.5 cm (8 inch) round, 7.5 cm (3 inch) deep cake tin with non-stick baking parchment. Preheat the oven to 180°C (350°F) Mark 4.

2 Fit the metal blade. Place the butter, sugar, flour, baking powder and eggs in the food processor. Add the grated rind of the lemon and 30 ml (2 tbsp) lemon juice. Process until just combined and smooth.

3 Spoon half the mixture into the bottom of the cases or tin. Spread the lemon curd evenly over the top and spoon the remaining cake mixture over the top to cover.

4 Bake for about 20 minutes, or 40 minutes for one large cake, until golden and firm to the touch. Transfer to a wire rack to cool. To serve, dust with icing sugar.

Vanilla Crumble Cakes

A quick and easy tray bake. A vanilla sponge is covered with a crumbly topping and baked until golden. It is served, cut into individual bars.

Preparation time: 15 minutes, plus cooling

Cooking time: 50-55 minutes

Cals per cake: 160

Makes 25 bars

250 g (9 oz) butter	**grated rind 1 lemon**
250 g (9 oz) caster sugar	**3 eggs, size 2**
125 g (4 oz) plain white flour	**7.5 ml (1½ tsp) vanilla essence**
175 g (6 oz) self-raising white flour	

1 Preheat the oven to 180°C (350°F) Mark 4. Grease and base-line a tin about 4 cm (1½ inch) deep, base measurement 26 x 15.5 cm (10¼ x 6½ inch).

2 Fit the metal blade. Place 75 g (3 oz) butter, cut into pieces in the food processor bowl with 75 g (3 oz) caster sugar. Process until smooth. Add the plain flour and process for 8-10 seconds until the mixture resembles very rough breadcrumbs. Transfer to a bowl and set aside.

3 Place the remaining 175 g (6 oz) butter, 175 g (6 oz) caster sugar, self-raising flour, grated lemon rind, eggs and vanilla essence in the food processor bowl. Process for 15 seconds or until smooth. Pour into the prepared tin.

4 Sprinkle the reserved crumble topping over the surface of the mixture and press down to cover. Bake for 50-55 minutes, covering loosely with foil, if necessary. Cool for 5 minutes before turning out onto a wire rack to cool.

5 Serve, cut into bars. Store in an airtight container for up to three days.

Chocolate Pecan Bars

A short biscuit base is topped with a chocolate chip and pecan nut sponge to make these tasty cakes. There is also a hidden chocolate and hazelnut layer through the centre.

Preparation time: 15 minutes, plus cooling

Cooking time: 1 hour

Cals per bar: 200

Makes 25

BASE
125 g (4 oz) plain white flour
25 g (1 oz) icing sugar
65 g (2½ oz) butter
1 egg yolk
TOPPING
75 g (3 oz) pecan nuts
125 g (4 oz) self-raising white flour

125 g (4 oz) caster sugar
125 g (4 oz) butter, softened
2 eggs, size 2
3-4 drops vanilla essence
150 g (5 oz) milk chocolate chips
90 ml (6 tbsp) chocolate and hazelnut spread, such as Nutella

1 Preheat the oven to 180°C (350°F) Mark 4. Grease and base-line a tin about 4 cm (1½ inch) deep, base measurement 26 x 15.5 cm (10¼ x 6½ inch).

2 Fit the metal blade. Place the flour, icing sugar and butter, cut into pieces in the food processor bowl. Process until the mixture resembles breadcrumbs. Add the egg yolk and process for 10-15 seconds or until the mixture begins to come together.

3 Turn into the tin and press into a thin layer to cover the base. Bake for 15 minutes, or until golden.

4 Meanwhile coarsely chop the pecan nuts using the metal blade. Transfer to a small bowl and set aside.

5 Place the self-raising flour, caster sugar, butter, eggs and vanilla essence in the food processor bowl. Process for 10-15 seconds or until smooth. Remove the blade and fold in the chocolate chips and chopped pecan nuts. Set aside.

6 Spread the chocolate and hazelnut spread over the cooked pastry base. Spread the cake mixture on top, to cover. Reduce the oven to 180°C (350°F) Mark 4 and bake for 45-50 minutes, or until golden. Cover loosely with foil, if necessary. Cool for about 10 minutes, before turning out onto a wire rack to cool.

7 Cut into about 25 bars and store in an airtight container for up to two days.

Coconut Bars

Creamed coconut is combined with vanilla to flavour these attractive biscuits. After baking, the ends are dipped in chocolate and toasted coconut.

Preparation time: 25 minutes, plus cooling
Cooking time: 10-12 minutes
Cals per biscuit: 150
Makes 20

75 g (3 oz) butter, softened	**2.5 ml (½ tsp) vanilla essence**
75 g (3 oz) creamed coconut	**5 ml (1 tsp) milk**
75 g (3 oz) caster sugar	**125 g (4 oz) white chocolate**
225 g (8 oz) plain white flour	**60 ml (4 tbsp) lightly toasted coconut**
1 egg	

1 Preheat oven to 180°C (350°F) Mark 4. Grease two baking sheets. Fit the food processor with the metal blade. Cut the butter into small pieces and add to the processor bowl. Add the creamed coconut, sugar, flour, egg, vanilla essence and milk.

2 Process all the ingredients for 45-60 seconds or until combined, adding sufficient milk to give a fairly soft consistency. Place the mixture in a piping bag fitted with a 1 cm (½ inch) star nozzle.

3 Pipe the mixture into finger shapes or 'S' shapes on to the prepared baking sheets, slightly spaced apart. Bake for 10-12 minutes, until pale golden.

4 Transfer to a wire rack to cool. Break the chocolate into small pieces and place in a bowl over simmering water to melt. Stir until smooth. Dip the ends of the biscuits in the chocolate and then the toasted coconut. Leave to set.

NOTE

Use the creamed coconut at room temperature. If it is hard, use the grating disc and grate into the food processor bowl before blending the biscuit ingredients together.

VARIATION

Instead of piping the biscuits, roll into walnut size balls and flatten slightly with a fork. Bake as above.

Banana and Chocolate Cookies

Chopped sun-dried bananas add a lovely flavour to homemade chunky oat cookies.
These bananas are readily available in health food stores.

Preparation time: 15 minutes, plus cooling
Cooking time: 12 minutes
Cals per biscuit: 175-150
Makes 24-28

125 g (4 oz) sun-dried bananas		**1 egg**	
200 g (7 oz) plain or milk chocolate		**125 g (4 oz) porridge oats**	
125 g (4 oz) unsalted butter		**150 g (5 oz) self-raising white flour**	
125 g (4 oz) light muscovado sugar			

1 Preheat the oven to 180°C (350°F) Mark 4. Lightly grease 2-3 baking sheets. Roughly cut the bananas into 2.5 cm (1 inch) lengths.

2 Fit the metal blade and finely chop the bananas. Remove and reserve. Chop the chocolate by hand, into small chunks.

3 Cut the butter into small pieces and place in the food processor with the sugar. Blend until creamy. Add the egg, oats and flour and blend until the mixture starts to bind together. If necessary scrape the mixture from the sides of the food processor bowl.

4 Add the chopped bananas and chocolate and process on pulse until incorporated into the mixture.

5 Take heaped dessertspoonfuls of the mixture and space them, slightly apart, on the prepared baking sheets. Bake for 12 minutes, or until light golden.

6 Transfer to a wire rack to cool. Store in an airtight container.

VARIATION

Use finely chopped dates in place of the bananas.

Malted Apple Scones

These lightly spiced, moist, nutty scones are lovely served warm with butter or even as a snack with cheese.

Preparation time: 15 minutes, plus cooling
Cooking time: 40-45 minutes
Cals per wedge: 185

Makes 8 wedges

1 large cooking apple, about 275 g (10 oz)	**pinch of ground cloves**
150 g (5 oz) malted granary flour	**40 g (1½ oz) butter**
150 g (5 oz) plain white flour	**25 g (1 oz) caster sugar**
pinch of salt	**50-75 ml (2-3 fl oz) milk**
12.5 ml (2½ tsp) baking powder	**milk, to glaze**
2.5 ml (½ tsp) ground cinnamon	**coarse sugar, to sprinkle**

1 Preheat the oven to 220°C (425°F) Mark 7. Lightly grease a baking sheet. Peel, core and quarter the apple.

2 Fit the metal blade. Place the malted granary flour, plain flour, salt, baking powder, cinnamon and cloves in the food processor and process for a few seconds to mix the dry ingredients together.

3 Cut the butter into pieces, add and process until blended. Add the sugar. Fit the grating disc and grate the apples.

4 Return the metal blade to the food processor. With the machine running add sufficient milk through the feed tube to give a soft dough.

5 Turn out onto a floured surface and shape into a dome. Transfer to the baking sheet and flatten slightly. Mark into 8 wedges with a floured knife.

6 Brush with milk, to glaze, and sprinkle with sugar. Bake for 20 minutes. Reduce the oven to 180°C (350°F) Mark 4 and bake for a further 20-25 minutes, until firm. Transfer to a wire rack to cool.

Rustic White Bread

This quantity makes sufficient for a 700 g (1½ lb) loaf. Check the amount of dough your processor can handle before starting.

Preparation time: 10 minutes, plus rising and cooling
Cooking time: 35 minutes
Cals per loaf: 1735
Makes 1 loaf

450 g (1 lb) strong plain white flour	**25 g (1 oz) butter**
5 ml (1 tsp) salt	**milk, to glaze**
5 ml (1 tsp) caster sugar	**poppy seeds, sesame seeds or coarse oatmeal, to sprinkle**
7.5 ml (1½ tsp) fast action dried yeast	

1 Fit the dough blade or hook. Add the flour, salt, sugar and yeast to the food processor and process for a few seconds to mix together.

2 Add the butter and process briefly to blend into the flour. With the processor running quickly pour 300 ml (½ pint) tepid water in through the feed tube. Within 15-20 seconds a ball of dough will start to form. Continue to process for a further 20-30 seconds.

3 Turn the dough onto a lightly floured surface and knead lightly. Shape into a long thick roll, working in a little more flour if the dough is very soft. Grease a baking sheet or 900 g (2 lb) loaf tin. Place the dough on the tray or in the tin.

4 Cover loosely with a tea towel and leave to rise for about 1 hour, or until doubled in size. Preheat the oven to 220°C (425°F) Mark 7.

5 Lightly brush the loaf with milk and scatter with the seeds. Slash the top with a sharp knife. Bake for 20 minutes. Reduce the temperature to 180°C (350°F) Mark 4 and bake for a further 15 minutes. To test, tap the base of the loaf, it should sound hollow. Transfer to a wire rack to cool.

VARIATIONS
Wholemeal bread: Use strong plain wholemeal flour or half strong plain white flour and half strong plain wholemeal flour.

Rolls: Divide the dough into 8 pieces and shape into rounds or ovals. Glaze with milk and scatter with seeds after rising. Bake for about 20 minutes at 220°C (425°F) Mark 7.

Focaccia

This light bread, is ideal as an accompaniment to soups, starters and casseroles. It is also perfect for sandwiches.

Preparation time: 30 minutes, plus rising and cooling
Cooking time: 20-25 minutes
Cals per serving: 275-210
Makes 2
Each serves 6-8

1 sachet fast action yeast	**450 ml (¾ pint) warm water**
pinch of sugar	**105 ml (7 tbsp) extra-virgin olive oil**
700 g (1½ lb) strong plain white flour	**coarse sea or crystal salt, for sprinkling**

1 Fit the dough blade or hook. Place the yeast, sugar and flour in the processor bowl. With the motor running add the water and 45 ml (3 tbsp) olive oil through the feed tube. Within 15-20 seconds a ball of dough will start to form. Continue to process for a further 20-30 seconds.

2 Turn the dough onto a lightly floured surface and knead lightly. If too soft to handle, knead in a little more flour. Place in a clean oiled bowl, cover with a damp tea towel and leave to rise for about 1 hour, or until doubled in size.

3 Lightly oil two shallow 25 cm (10 inch) metal pizza or pie plates. Knock back the dough and divide in half. Shape each piece into a round ball on a floured surface and roll out into a 25 cm (10 inch) circle. Place in the oiled tins. Cover with a damp tea-towel and leave to rise for 30 minutes.

4 Remove the tea-towel and, using your fingertips, make deep dimples all over the surface of the dough. Cover and leave to rise once more until double in size, about 1 hour.

5 Preheat the oven to 200°C (400°F) Mark 6. Drizzle over the remaining oil and sprinkle generously with salt. Spray with water and bake for 20-25 minutes. Spray with water twice during cooking. Transfer to a wire rack to cool. Eat the same day or freeze as soon as it is cool.

VARIATIONS

Olive and Sun-dried Tomato Focaccia : Drain 50 g (2 oz) sun-dried tomatoes in oil, slice and knead into the dough at stage 2. Sprinkle the dough with black or green olives at stage 5.

Sage and Onion Focaccia: Chop 20 sage leaves and knead into the dough at stage 2. Peel 2 small red onions and cut in half. Using the slicing disc, thinly slice. Sprinkle over the dough with extra sage leaves at stage 5.

Walnut Stollen

A freshly blended walnut paste takes the place of the more traditional marzipan in this sweet festive bread. Serve warm or lightly toasted.

Preparation time: 25 minutes, plus rising and cooling
Cooking time: 40 minutes
Cals per slice: 400-340
Makes 12-14 slices

125 g (4 oz) unsalted butter	75 g (3 oz) walnut pieces
150 ml (¼ pint) milk	50 g (2 oz) raisins
1 egg	50 g (2 oz) sultanas
400 g (14 oz) strong plain white flour	**WALNUT PASTE**
1.25 ml (¼ tsp) salt	125 g (4 oz) walnut pieces
2.5 ml (½ tsp) ground mixed spice	50 g (2 oz) caster sugar
10 ml (2 tsp) fast action dried yeast	50 g (2 oz) icing sugar
50 g (2 oz) caster sugar	1 egg yolk
40 g (1½ oz) glacé cherry pieces	icing sugar, for dusting

1 Melt the butter in a small saucepan. Stir in the milk and egg. Fit the dough blade. Place the flour, salt, mixed spice, yeast and sugar in the food processor. Process for a few seconds to mix together.

2 With the processor running, quickly pour the milk mixture through the feed tube. Within 15-20 seconds a ball of dough will start to form. Continue to process for a further 30 seconds. Turn onto a lightly floured surface and knead lightly. Place in a clean oiled bowl, cover and leave to rise in a warm place for 1 hour, or until doubled in size.

3 Make the walnut paste. Fit the metal blade and process the walnuts until ground. Add the sugars and egg yolk and blend until the mixture starts to bind together. Knead into a ball.

4 Lightly grease a baking sheet. Turn the dough onto a lightly floured surface and knead in the cherries, walnuts, raisins and sultanas. Roll out the dough into a 30 x 20 cm (12 x 8 inch) rectangle.

5 Shape the walnut paste into a 28 cm (11 inch) sausage and lay down the centre of the dough. Fold the dough over the paste to enclose it and press down.

6 Transfer to the prepared baking sheet and cover loosely. Leave in a warm place for 20-30 minutes, until well risen. Preheat oven to 190°C (375°F) Mark 5.

7 Bake for 35-40 minutes, until golden and the bread sounds hollow when tapped on the base. Transfer to a wire rack to cool. Serve dusted with icing sugar.